Richard Parry

An Attempt to Demonstrate the Messiahship of Jesus

From the prophetic history and chronology of Messiah's kingdom in Daniel

Richard Parry

An Attempt to Demonstrate the Messiahship of Jesus
From the prophetic history and chronology of Messiah's kingdom in Daniel

ISBN/EAN: 9783337164799

Printed in Europe, USA, Canada, Australia, Japan

Cover: Foto ©Lupo / pixelio.de

More available books at **www.hansebooks.com**

A N

ATTEMPT

TO DEMONSTRATE THE

MESSIAHSHIP of JESUS,

FROM THE

PROPHETIC HISTORY AND CHRONOLOGY OF

MESSIAH's kingdom in DANIEL.

By RICHARD PARRY, D.D.

Preacher at Market-Harborough.

"Whoso readeth [Daniel THE Prophet] let
him underftand."   Jesus.

LONDON:

Printed by J. and W. OLIVER in Bartholomew-Clofe:

And Sold by LOCKYER DAVIS in Holborn,

Printer to the Royal Society.

M DCC LXXVI.

Sir JOHN PRINGLE, Baronet.

S I R,

SOME years ago you were pleafed
to requeft of the celebrated Profeffor
at GOETTINGEN a faithful, and, what
he thought, a true verfion of Daniel's
prophecy concerning the Seventy
Weeks. He inftantly replied, without
the leaft deliberation, that he could
not poffibly give one. His reafon then
was, that the received reading is fuf-
picious. And he has fince fent you
his doubts about this famous prophecy,
inftead of a verfion of it.

Sequeftered

Sequeſtered from the learned, and from books, (except ſuch as my own little library ſupplies me with) I have been forced to take the prophecy as I found it ; and I have endeavoured to give a good account of it. I wiſh, Sir, it may afford you any ſatisfaction, as the prophecy ſeems to have been an object of your attention. It will not appear with leſs advantage, by being connected with the other two. For theſe prophecies, joined together, form ſuch a threefold cord as, I truſt, will not be quickly broken.

I have, Sir, the honor to be, with the greateſt reſpect,

Your moſt humble
and moſt obedient ſervant,

RI. PARRY.

ADVERTISEMENT.

THE following papers contain nothing more than what the title expreſſes, " an ATTEMPT to demonſtrate the Meſſiahſhip of Jeſus," a faint ſketch, or rude outline, which might perhaps be filled up and perfected by ſome happier writer, of greater abilities, more leiſure, and better health for ſtudies of this nature.

The ARGUMENT employed is the argument from PROPHECY, a medium of proof peculiarly, though not excluſively, addreſſed to the JEWS. " To them were committed the oracles of God," and they apply moſt of, if not all the prophecies, which we do, to MESSIAH. The only diſpute is about the SENSE, that is, whether they are to be underſtood in a TEMPORAL or a SPIRITUAL ſenſe. And one would think, that, after the experience of SEVENTEEN CENTURIES, little more than a common underſtanding, with the aſſiſtance of common integrity, were requiſite to decide the controverſy.

The

The prophecies, attempted to be explained and illustrated, are confessedly of the greatest importance. They have been pressed into the service of every writer, of every party. But party is the bane of religious truth. And if the author of these papers has succeeded in his attempt, the success is to be imputed, solely, to his freedom from party, and prejudice, and prepossession.

PAPISTS and PROTESTANTS, as such, are out of the question. The dispute is, here, confined to JEWS and CHRISTIANS. And if it shall appear, that the FALL OF PAGANISM, throughout the ROMAN empire, is fairly predicted in the first prophecy, the FALL OF JEWDAISM in the second, the very TIME of the fall of Jewdaism in the third, and that JESUS was the author of those great events; it is hoped, that every capable and candid inquirer will join in the necessary conclusion, That "THE TESTIMONY OF JESUS IS THE SPIRIT OF PROPHECY."

INTRO-

INTRODUCTION.

THE great evidences to the truth of Chriſtianity are prophecies and miracles. The miracles which Jeſus wrought, are unqueſtionable proofs, that He was a teacher ſent from God. And the prophecies, fulfilled in Jeſus, are unqueſtionable proofs likewiſe, that He was the Meſſiah foretold to be ſent, in due time, into the world. For if Jeſus did the works which no man ever did, and if He fulfilled the law and the prophets, which no other man did ; What pretence can the Jew and the Deiſt have for diſputing his miſſion or his Meſſiahſhip ?

Prophecies are not neceſſary credentials to a divine commiſſion. For who prophecied of Moſes ? And yet his authority was ſufficiently eſtabliſhed by miracles. But Jeſus offered himſelf to the Jewiſh

nation

nation as their Meſſiah foretold by Moſes and the prophets. He muſt therefore neceſſarily appeal to the evidence of prophecy. Miracles alone would be, in his caſe, inſufficient. For if Jeſus did not anſwer to the characters of the Meſſiah given by the prophets, all his miracles could never prove him to be the Meſſiah?

It is therefore incumbent on the rational advocate for Chriſtianity to ſhew the completion of the Meſſiah-character in the perſon of Jeſus [1.] With this view I have undertaken an explanation of ſome very important predictions. I have endeavoured, with the ſtricteſt impartiality, to find out their true meaning. And I now offer the reſult of my inquiry as an ESSAY towards ſtrengthening the great argument from prophecy for the truth of Chriſtianity.

KINGDOM of HEAVEN;

OR, THE

FALL of PAGANISM.

Nebuchadnezzar's Dream.	Daniel's Interpretation.
A GREAT IMAGE.	[PAGANISM.]
Its HEAD of fine GOLD,	THOU THYSELF art the HEAD of GOLD.
Its BREAST and ARMS of SILVER,	After thee will arife ANOTHER empire.
Its BELLY and THIGHS of BRASS,	Then a THIRD empire.
Its LEGS of IRON,	Then a FOURTH empire will be ftrong as iron, forafmuch as iron breaketh in pieces and fubdueth all [metals]; and, as iron that breaketh all thofe [metals], it will break in pieces and bruife [all nations].
Its FEET part of	And whereas thou faweft FEET and TOES, part of

Nebuchadnezzar's Dream continued.	Daniel's Interpretation continued.
IRON and part of CLAY.	potter's clay, and part of iron, the empire will be DIVIDED [into TEN kingdoms or provinces], and there will be in IT [in each division] of the ROOT of iron, forasmuch as thou sawest IRON mixed with clay. And as the TOES of the FEET were part of IRON and part of CLAY, so A KINGDOM will be partly STRONG and partly BRITTLE. And whereas thou sawest iron MIXED with clay, they will MINGLE themselves with the seed of men [the Romans with the provincialists], but they will not cleave one to another, even as the iron did not mix with the clay [so as to cleave to it].
A STONE was cut out without hands, and it smote the image upon its FEET of iron and clay, and brake them to pieces. Then was the iron, the clay, the brass, the silver, and the gold, broken to pieces together, and they became like the chaff of the summer threshing floors, and the wind carried them	In the days of these kings the God of heaven will set up a KINGDOM which shall never be destroyed; and the kingdom shall not be left to other people, but it shall break in pieces and consume all these kingdoms, and it shall stand for ever; forasmuch as thou sawest that a STONE was cut out of a mountain without hands,

Nebuchadnezzar's Dream continued.	Daniel's Interpretation continued.
away, that no place was found for them ; and the ſtone that ſmɔte the image became a great mountain, and filled the whole earth.	and that it brake in pieces the iron, the braſs, the clay, the ſilver, and the gold.

DANIEL II. 1——45.

Every thing in theſe exhibitions is ſo ſtrongly marked, and ſo accurately diſtinguiſhed, that it requires ſome pains, and more ſubtilty, to miſtake the meaning. The KING, for the dream was ſent to him in that character, " had been thinking upon his bed what would come to paſs hereafter." By comparing this remark with the dream itſelf, which was intended to be an anſwer to his thoughts, and " to make known to the king what was to come to paſs," we may ſafely affirm, that this mighty prince had been conſidering the future fates or fortunes of HIMSELF, his EMPIRE, and its RELIGION ; whether BABYLON would always continue " THE GOLDEN CITY, THE LADY OF KINGDOMS *," and whether HE HIMSELF might not hereafter be inroiled in the ſacred canon of divinities, and repreſented,

B 3

---

* Iſaiah xiv. 4. Chap. xlvii. 5.

fented, as an object of worfhip, by a
GOLDEN IMAGE [2]. Full of thefe pleafing,
flattering thoughts, he fell afleep; when
God vouchfafed him, for his inftruction,
a prophetic dream, fuited and adapted to
his fituation and circumftances. The
dream alarmed him, for it was more than
common; " his fpirit was troubled, and
his fleep broke from him." In this anxiety
and diftrefs, he gave orders for the whole
tribe of ftate-jugglers to be called together, " the magicians, the aftrologers,
and the forcerers, and the Chaldeans, to
fhew the king his dreams." He immediately acquaints them with the occafion
of his fending for them. " I have dream-
ed a dream, and my fpirit is troubled to
know the dream." The Chaldeans faid
to the king, " Tell thy fervants the dream,
and we will fhew the interpretation." He
anfwered, with great addrefs [3], " The
thing is gone from me. If ye will not make
known unto me the dream, with the interpretation, 'ye fhall be cut in pieces, and
your houfes fhall be made a dunghill.
But if ye fhew the dream, and the interpretation thereof, ye fhall receive of me
gifts, and rewards, and great honor."
They

They anfwered again, " Let the king tell his fervants the dream, and we will fhew the interpretation of it." The king replied, " I know of certainty that ye would gain time, becaufe ye fee the thing is gone from me. But if ye will not make known unto me the dream, there is but one decree for you ; for ye have prepared lying and corrupt words to fpeak before me, till the time be changed. Therefore tell me the dream, and I fhall know that ye can fhew me the interpretation thereof." It was not poffible to put the matter upon a fairer iffue. ONEIROCRITICISM, or the interpreting of dreams, was a very confiderable part of pagan divination. Now common fenfe will readily inform any man, who will condefcend to liften to it, that, without infpiration, there can be no true interpreting of prophetic dreams ; and that with infpiration, which all diviners pretended to, the dreams themfelves may be as eafily known as their meaning. " Tell me therefore the dream, faid the king to his diviners, and I fhall know that ye can fhew me the interpretation thereof." The Chaldeans replied, " There is not a man upon the earth that can fhew the king's matter; therefore there is no king, lord, nor ruler that afked fuch things of any magician, or aftrologer, or Chaldean. And it is a rare thing that the king requireth, and there is none other that can fhew it before the king, except the Gods whofe dwelling is not with flefh." After this frank declaration, "the king was angry and very furious, and commanded to deftroy all the wife-men of Babylon," without exception, as cheats and impoftors. "So a decree went forth, that the wife-men fhould be flain."

Daniel, it feems, and his three countrymen were unknown to the king [4], for he called and confulted the Chaldeans [5] only. But when the decree went forth for the deftruction of all the wife-men, then "they fought Daniel and his fellows to be flain" likewife. The prophet, who was totally unacquainted with every thing that had happened, addreffed himfelf "with counfel and wifdom to the captain of the guard," who was intrufted with the execution of the fatal edict, and inquired into the caufe of it. "Why," fays he, upon what, or whofe account, "is a decree fo hafty from the king? The officer,
                                              with

with great attention and politenefs (for
Daniel, though a captive, was of the royal
family of Judah) informed him of the
whole bufinefs ; and, with equal huma-
nity, permitted him to go in to the king
" to defire time" till the next day, when
" he would fhew him" both the dream
and " the interpretation." At the time
appointed (" the fecret" having been pre-
vioufly " revealed to Daniel," at his ear-
neft requeft, " in a night-vifion)," he was
introduced to the king, and faid, " The
fecret, which the king hath demanded,
cannot the wife-men, the aftrologers, the
magicians, the foothfayers, fhew unto the
king. But there is a God in heaven that
revealeth fecrets, and maketh known to
king Nebuchadnezzar what fhall come to
pafs hereafter. As for me," continues the
prophet, with the greateft modefty, " this
fecret is not revealed to me for any wifdom that I have more than any living,
but for their fakes," his own and his brethren and companions' fake, " who fhall
make known the interpretation to the
king, and that thou mayeft know the
thoughts of thy heart.

Thou,

Thou, O king, faweft, and behold! A GREAT IMAGE. This great image, whofe brightnefs was excellent, ftood before thee, and the form thereof was terrible." The image, I conceive, afcended gradually out of the earth, according to the fucceffion of its component parts, till at length it ftood upon its feet, a huge formidable Co-LOSSUS, the exprefs reprefentative of PA-GANISM, tyrannizing in four fucceffive em-pires, and perfecuting the church of God.

As the Coloffus itfelf is the image of paganifm, or falfe religion, fo the four METALS of which it was compofed de-note fo many diftinct NATIONS, and its fucceffive PARTS, the fucceffive EMPIRES of thofe nations. The firft in order, and which was then exifting, was the BABYLO-NIAN. " THOU THYSELF * art the HEAD OF GOLD." That is, the KING of BABYLON was fo; for it follows,

" And after THEE," not perfonally but politically, " fhall arife ANOTHER EMPIRE, inferior to thee." This was the MEDO-PERSIAN. Our prophet, who lived to fee the fall of the Babylonian empire, exprefsly tells us, that then " DARIUS THE MEDIAN took

* אתה הוא —— See the London Polyglott.

took the empire †," according to the prophecy given to Belſhazzar, " Thy kingdom is divided, and given to the MEDES and Perſians ‡." And from that time to the reign of Cyrus, the Babylonians were ſubject to " the laws of the MEDES and Perſians ‖," which are afterwards called " the laws of the PERSIANS and Medes §."

" Then another, a THIRD EMPIRE OF BRASS." This was ₌the empire of the GREEKS or MACEDONIANS. The Greeks, we know, were ſtyled χαλκοχίτωνες, braſen-coated. But I lay no ſtreſs on this circumſtance, nor indeed ought any ſtreſs to be laid upon it, for braſs cannot repreſent braſs [6]. It is more material to obſerve, with the prophet, that the third empire was to " bear rule over all the earth," exactly as Alexander himſelf and the hiſtorians deſcribe it. Juſtin ſays, that Alexander, " having at length received the empire, commanded that he ſhould be called the king of ALL *the* EARTH, even
of

---

† Dan. v. 31.   ‡ Dan. v. 28.

‖ Dan. vi. 8, 12, 15.

§ Eſther i. 19. So ver. 3. " the power of PERSIA and Media;" and ver. 18. " the ladies of PERSIA and Media."

of the world * ;" for, as Arrian obferves, " he feemed to himfelf and to his friends to be lord both of all the earth and fea §."

The next empire in fucceffion was the ROMAN, which is thus prophetically delineated. " Then a FOURTH empire will be ftrong as IRON, forafmuch as iron breaketh in pieces and fubdueth all" metals ; " and as iron that breaketh all thofe, it will break in pieces and bruife " all the people reprefented by them. Nothing could be more truly characteriftic of the Romans, than the metal which formed the LEGS of the ftatue. They were indeed an IRON race, breaking in pieces the gold, the filver, and the brafs, and reducing them to dirt ; that is, bringing the nations, reprefented by thofe metals, into the loweft and vileft fubjection. " Plunderers of the world ! as Galgacus the Britifh general ftyles them, When lands fail before the deftroyers of all things, they ranfack even the fea. If an enemy is rich, they are covetous of his wealth ; if poor, ambitious

of

---

* " Accepto deinde imperio, regem fe terrarum omnium, ac mundi, appellari poffit." Idem lib. 12. c. 16. § 9.

§ Αυτον τι αυτω Αλιξανδρον κ) τοις αμφ' αυτον φαιριαι γης τι απασης κ) θαλασσης κυριοι De exped. Alex. lib. 7. c. 14.

of his dominion; whom neither the eaft nor the weft can fatisfy. They alone defire with equal affection both riches and poverty. Pilfering, flaughtering, plundering under falfe pretences, is in their opinion empire; and where they make a folitude, they call it peace *."

From the Romans themfelves the prophet paffes to their pagan kingdoms or provinces, placed, with the moft exquifite propriety, under the iron legs of their mafters. " Whereas thou faweft the feet and TOES, part of potter's clay and part of iron, the empire will be DIVIDED," or diftributed, into as many kingdoms as the toes upon the feet of the image [7]. Hence ROME is ftyled by the Jews " DOMINA DIGITORUM," that is, without a figure, " the LADY OF KINGDOMS;" or, in the language of St John, " that great city; which REIGNETH over the KINGS, the KINGDOMS, of the

* " Raptores orbis ! Poftquam cuncta vaftantibus defuere terræ, et mare fcrutantur. Si locuples hoftis eft, avari; fi pauper, ambitiofi; quos non oriens, non occidens fatiaverit. Soli omnium opes atque inopiam pari affectu concupifcunt. Auferre, trucidare, rapere falfis nominibus, imperium; atque ubi folitudinem faciunt, pacem appellant." Tac. vita Agric. f. 30.

the earth †." " And there will be in IT," in each divifion, implied in the term DIVIDED[8], " of the root of [9]" the nation reprefented by " the IRON, forafmuch as thou faweft IRON mixed with miry clay." This feems to fignify, that for the better fecuring of the provinces, and keeping of them in fubjection to their mafters, a proportionable number of Roman legions would be ftationed in each divifion; or that Roman merchants would fettle among the provincialifts for the fake of trade and commerce. " And as the TOES were part of IRON and part of CLAY, fo A KINGDOM," each kingdom or province reprefented by a toe, " will be partly STRONG and partly BRITTLE." Though every kingdom or province would be, in part, firmly united to the parent country, juft as the iron part of each toe was firmly united to the leg from whence it derived its exiftence, yet would it likewife, in another

† Rev. xvii. 18. Ἡ πολις ἡμεγαλη, ἡ εχουσα ΒΑΣΙΛΕΙΑΝ επι των ΒΑΣΙΛΕΩΝ της γης. Thefe were THE KINGDOMS OF THIS WORLD, which were difplayed by the tempter in all their glory to the bleffed Jefus, and which he then greatly rejected, and afterwards difclaimed, when he witneffed that good confeffion before Pontius Pilate, " MY KINGDOM IS NOT OF THIS WORLD."

another part, be brittle, crumbling like clay, and ready to fall away upon every occafion of difcontent, and oftentimes without any. " And whereas thou faweft iron MIXED with miry clay, they will MIX themfelves with the feed of " private" men; but they will not cleave one to another, even as the iron was not mixed with the clay," fo as to cleave to it. This perhaps may mean, that the Romans will inter-marry with the provincialifts; the lords of the world, as they proudly ftyled them-felves, with their vaffals. But even this natural principle of union and agreement, will not be powerful enough to prevent variance and diffention; the luft of rule and dominion being more prevalent than all the fofter affections.

· " And in the days of thefe kings will the GOD OF HEAVEN SET UP A KINGDOM which fhall never be deftroyed; and the kingdom fhall not be left to other people, but it fhall break in pieces and confume all thefe kingdoms, and it fhall ftand for ever; forafmuch as thou faweft that a STONE was cut out of a MOUNTAIN with-out hands, and that it brake in pieces the iron, the brafs, the clay, the filver, and the gold;"

gold," and succeeded into the place of the image.

KINGS, as the prophet himself has more than once explained his meaning, are here put for KINGDOMS. And by THESE kingdoms we are to understand ROME and her pagan PROVINCES; the Jewish writers calling every kind of government, whether sovereign or dependent, by the common name of kingdom. " IN THE DAYS OF THESE kings SHALL THE GOD OF HEAVEN SET UP A KINGDOM." Accordingly the heir to his kingdom was born in the reign of " Cæsar AUGUSTUS [10]." And " in the fifteenth year of the reign of TIBERIUS Cæsar, came John the baptist preaching in the wilderness of Jewdea, and saying, Repent ye, for THE KINGDOM OF HEAVEN IS AT HAND*." And when the baptist had fulfilled his course, Jesus began his ministry in the same manner, " preaching the gospel of THE KINGDOM OF GOD †." The other empires had been set up by human craft, and human power; by the stratagems of politicians, and the strength of armies. But THIS kingdom was to be solely the work of God, as the stone was

cut

* Matt. iii. 2. † Mark i. 14.

cut out of the mountain, " Jerufalem, the holy mountain," WITHOUT HANDS. Daniel himfelf ufes the word " hand" elfewhere in the fame fenfe. Speaking of Antiochus Epiphanes under the image of " a little horn," he fays, " he fhall be broken without hand *," he fhall be deftroyed neither in anger nor in battle, but by the vengeance of God. The Jews feem to have ufed this expreffion proverbially, to denote any thing MIRACULOUS. Our Saviour had faid, " Deftroy this temple," meaning the temple of his body, " and in three days I will raife it up." The comment of the Jews was, " I will deftroy this temple," the temple of Jerufalem, " that is made WITH HANDS, and within three days I will build another made WITHOUT HANDS †." Thus " the ftone was cut out of the mountain without hands." The king faw the axe, but the hand that hewed therewith was invifible. And in like manner the Chriftian church was feparated from the Jewifh by the fecret power and operation of the holy fpirit. The apoftles were indeed the vifible inftruments in this great

C   work

* Dan. viii. 25.   † Mark xiv. 58.

work. Some planted, others watered; but God alone gave the increafe.

" This kingdom fhall never be deftroyed, nor left to other people." The BABYLONIAN empire was deftroyed, and left to the Perfians; the PERSIAN was deftroyed, and left to the Macedonians; the MACEDONIAN was deftroyed, and left to the Romans. But THIS kingdom, the kingdom of the God of heaven, fhall never be deftroyed, nor left to other people. It fhall not be fucceeded by a new EMPIRE; no FAMILY, nor any other political, COMPACT fhall fo far prevail, as to fet up a fixth UNIVERSAL monarchy. So far from being itfelf deftroyed, " it fhall break in pieces and confume all thefe kingdoms," all the pagan kingdoms of the fourth empire---Rome herfelf and her provinces. " The kingdom of heaven," as the phrafe implies, and as the lord of the kingdom has exprefsly declared, " is not of this world;" and therefore the terms " breaking and confuming" muft be underftood accordingly. The Jews indeed, ever devoted to the low and little concerns of this life, fondly expected a temporal kingdom, a fifth monarchy to

be

be erected upon the ruins of the fourth; and Jerufalem to be the metropolis of the empire. But, behold the reverfe of their vain expectations! At the very time when they were looking for the Meffiah to fubdue the nations, " to bind their kings in chains, and their nobles in links of iron," even then they themfelves were broken in pieces and confumed, and their city and temple deftroyed by the Romans; and " THE WICKED ROMAN," as they delight to fpeak, is ftill remaining. If plain and obvious FACTS will not open people's eyes, and change their fentiments, it is hard to fay what will. And yet there is another FACT, the completion of this prophecy, which muft be, at leaft, equally convincing to every unprejudiced inquirer. The mountain is the Jewifh church; the ftone, cut out of that mountain, is the infant kingdom of God, or church of Chrift, extracted from the Jewifh. The Jews themfelves acknowledge, that " the ftone reprefents the Meffiah;" that is, agreeably with the ftyle of the prophecy, the Meffiah's kingdom. And they will do well to obferve, that the ftone cut out of the mountain, and not the mountain

itfelf;

itfelf, was to demolifh the image; or, in
other words, that the Meffiah's kingdom,
extracted from the Jewifh, and not the
Jewifh kingdom itfelf, was to atchieve
what is here predicted.   As the ftone was
homogeneal with the mountain [11], from
whence it was hewn, fo was the Chriftian
church with the Jewifh, from whence it
derived its exiftence.   They were indeed
effentially the fame.   One believed in A
MESSIAH TO COME, the other acknowledged him in the perfon of JESUS; and
THE MESSIAHSHIP OF JESUS IS THE
FOUNDATION OF THE GOSPEL [12]. " The
ftone fmote the image, the reprefentative
of paganifm, on its FEET of iron and clay,
and brake them to pieces."   That is, according to Daniel, " the kingdom of God
fhall break in pieces and confume all the
kingdoms" of the earth; or, in other
words, the true and undefiled religion of
Chrift fhall prevail over and deftroy the
falfe and idolatrous religions of the Roman
empire; all men fhall " willingly offer
themfelves," and become fubjects of the
great King.   As foon as the ftone fmote
the image upon its feet, it brake them in
pieces, and inlarged itfelf by an acceffion.

of

of thofe new materials. " The iron, the clay, the brafs, the filver, and the gold, were broken to pieces together [13], and became like the chaff of the fummer threfhing-floors, and the wind carried them away, that no place was found for them." And as foon as the apoftles addreffed themfelves to the converfion of the Gentiles, they made amazing havock in the provinces, and, in token of their conquefts, gave the conquered a new name; for, as St Luke obferves, in honor of his native city, " the difciples were called by divine appointment [14] CHRISTIANS firft in Antioch," the capital of Syria, which implies that they were afterwards called fo elfewhere. The prophet is not fpeaking of the deftruction of the empire in a phyfical, but in a moral fenfe. " The weapons of our warfare," fays the illuftrious apoftle to the Gentiles, who well knew both their nature and their ufe, " are not carnal, but fpiritual." The Romans therefore were not to be confumed, but converted; the pagans were to be deftroyed, and not the men; the only army to be flain was the " noble army of martyrs." Sent forth " like fheep into the midft of wolves;" the apoftles

went

went forth, in the spirit of simplicity, humility, and meekness, armed only with truth and innocence, the goodness of their cause, and the power of their God. And with these weapons they fought, prevailed, and conquered. So that before two cen-turies were run out, the provinces, the cities, the courts, the camps, were all full of Christians; and within less than three, from its first publication, the religion of Jesus became the religion of the empire. " The stone" (that " little flock," as the good shepherd once pathetically called it) went on " from strength to strength, in-creasing with the increase of God," till at length, by converting the materials of the image into itself, it " became a great mountain, and filled the whole earth." The Jewish church (the mountain from whence the stone was taken) was compa-ratively very small, and confined to one obscure corner of the Roman empire. But the stone (the Christian church) spread, with an irresistible progress, from east to west, grew into an exceeding great mountain which filled the whole of it. In this manner did the kingdom of the God of heaven break in pieces and con-

fume

fume all the pagan kingdoms of the fourth monarchy. " It came upon the princes as upon mortar, and as the potter treadeth clay. All kings fell down before it, all nations did it fervice." And thus the bleffed JESUS, the fon of the higheft, was conftituted in SPIRITUALS, what CÆSAR was in TEMPORALS, " KING OF KINGS, AND LORD OF LORDS."

Thus far, at leaft, we may venture to fay, with Daniel, " the dream is certain, and the interpretation thereof is fure." Neither the one nor the other is the mere fport of the imagination and fancy, for in every part the event has verified the prediction ; and there cannot poffibly be a ftronger atteftation to the truth of any prophecy than its accomplifhment. We have feen the kingdom of the ftone, and we have feen the empire of the mountain. We may therefore fecurely truft the remaining part in the hands of God. This kingdom " fhall ftand for ever." It has already ftood, to the aftonifhment of every ferious obferver ! almoft eighteen hundred years. The pagan empires were " of the earth earthy," and therefore of no long continuance. The Babylonian was de-

ftroyed

ſtroyed by the Perſians, the Perſian by the Macedonians, the Macedonian by the Ro-mans; and at laſt the Roman empire was ſwallowed up and loſt in the church of Chriſt. But this ſhall never be deſtroyed. It ſhall ſtand, in the ſtricteſt ſenſe, FOR EVER. The kingdom of GRACE ſhall be commenſurate with the exiſtence of the preſent world, and the kingdom of GLORY with that of the world to come. For as the LORD'S THRONE is in HEAVEN, neither the powers of EARTH nor of HELL SHALL BE EVER ABLE TO PREVAIL AGAINST IT.

We have now examined, in a curſory manner, the rich contents of this manifold prediction, and have viewed the gradual completion of all its parts. We have ſeen the FOUR great empires of the world ſuc-ceſſively riſing and falling, and yielding to a new maſter. We have ſeen too, which is the capital object intended, a FIFTH empire, called THE KINGDOM OF THE GOD OF HEAVEN, emerging from the moſt ob-ſcure corner of the Roman territories, wading through a bloody ſea of troubles, and at length triumphing over the powers of paganiſm, " leading captivity captive," and

and fixing the facred ftandard of the CROSS [15] in every part of the empire --- and the fcene of the prophecy extends no farther. Here then we too will clofe the fcene, only obferving, that a time will come when the Chriftian church will be both inlarged and purified. I cannot better defcribe this happy change of men and manners, than in the expreffive language of the evangelical prophet. " The wolf fhall dwell with the LAMB, and the LEOPARD fhall lie down with the KID, and the CALF and the young LION and the FATLING together, and a little CHILD fhall lead them. Even the cow and the BEAR fhall feed, their young ones fhall lie down to-gether, and the LION fhall eat ftraw like the ox. And the SUCKING child fhall play on the hole of the ASP, and the WEANED child fhall put his hand on the COCKATRICE's den. THEY SHALL NOT HURT NOR DESTROY IN ALL MY HOLY MOUNTAIN; FOR THE EARTH SHALL BE FULL OF THE KNOWLEDGE OF THE LORD, AS THE WATERS COVER THE SEA *."

* Ifaiah xi. 6—9.

THE

THE

KINGDOM OF HEAVEN;

OR, THE

FALL OF JEWDAISM.

Daniel's Vision.	The Angel's Interpre-tation.
Behold! the four winds of the heaven strove upon the great sea, and FOUR GREAT WILD-BEASTS came up from the sea, diverse one from another.	
The FIRST was like a LION, and had eagle's wings. I beheld till the wings thereof were plucked, wherewith it had been lifted up from the earth, and it was made to stand upon two feet as a man, and a man's heart was given to it.	
And, behold! another wild-beast, a SECOND like to a BEAR, and it raised up itself on one side. and it had three ribs in its mouth between its teeth; and they said thus to it, Arise, devour much flesh.	

Daniel's Vision continued. | **The Angel's Interpretation.**

After this I beheld, and, lo ! ANOTHER like a LEOPARD, which had on its back four wings of a fowl ; the wild-beaft had alfo four heads, and dominion was given to it.

After this, behold ! a FOURTH wild-beaft, dreadful and terrible, and ftrong exceedingly, and it had great iron teeth; and it devoured and brake in pieces and ftamped the refidue with its feet; and it was a copy of all the wild-beafts that were before it, and it had TEN HORNS.

I confidered the horns, and, behold ! there had come up among them ANOTHER, A LITTLE HORN, before whom three of the firft horns were plucked up; and, behold ! in this horn were eyes like the eyes of a man, but a mouth fpeaking great things.

I beheld till two thrones were placed, and the antient of days——the judge did fit, and the books were opened.

I beheld then, becaufe of the voice of the great words which the horn fpake, till A BEAST was flain,

Daniel's Vision continued.	The Angel's Interpretation.
and its BODY deftroyed, and given to the burning flame. As to the REST, [the remains,] of the beaft, their dominion was taken away, but their lives were prolonged for a feafon and time.	
I faw, and, behold! the likenefs of A SON OF MAN came upon the clouds of heaven, and came to the ANTIENT OF DAYS and was brought near before him. And he gave him dominion, and glory, and a kingdom, that ALL people, nations, and languages fhall ferve him. His dominion is an everlafting dominion, which fhall not be taken away, and his kingdom that which fhall not be deftroyed.	
I Daniel was grieved in my fpirit in the midft of my body, and the vifions of my head troubled me.	
I went near unto one of them that ftood by, and afked him the truth of all this.	
So he told me. and made me know the interpretation of the things.	
	Thofe GREAT WILD-BEASTS, namely, thofe FOUR.
	FOUR EMPIRES fuccef-fively arife out of the earth.

Daniel's Vision continued.

Then I would know the truth of the FOURTH wild-beast, which was copied from all the others, exceeding dreadful, whose teeth were of iron, and its nails of brass, which devoured, brake in pieces, and stamped the residue with its feet;

And of the TEN HORNS that were in its head;

And of the OTHER which had come up, and before whom three fell, even of that horn that had eyes, and a mouth that spake very great things, whose look was more stout than his fellows.

I had looked, and the same horn made war with the SAINTS, and prevailed against them, until the antient of days came, and gave judgment for the saints, that the time was come that the saints should possess the kingdom.

The Angel's Interpretion continued.

Then the SAINTS OF THE MOST HIGH shall receive the kingdom, and possess the kingdom for ever, even for ever and ever.

The FOURTH wild-beast.

A FOURTH empire will arise out of the earth, which will be copied from all the empires, and will devour

Daniel's Vision continued. | **The Angel's Interpretation continued.**

the whole earth, and tread it down, and break it in pieces.

And the TEN HORNS.

Out of this empire TEN kings will arise ; then ANOTHER will arise after them, and he will be diverse from the first ; then three kings will be subdued ; and he will speak great words against the most high, and will wear out the saints of the most high, and think to change times and laws ; and they shall be given into his hand until a time, and two-times, and the half of a time. Then the judge will sit, and they shall take away his dominion, to consume and to destroy it at the end.

And the kingdom and dominion, and the greatness of the kingdom under the whole heaven, shall be given to a people, the saints of the most high, whose kingdom is an everlasting kingdom, and all dominions shall serve and obey him.

Then shall be an end of the matter.

DANIEL VII. 1—28.

As

As in the former vifion Nebuchadnezzar, a PAGAN prince, faw the deftruction
of PAGANISM, fo here Daniel, a JEWISH
prophet, faw the deftruction of JEWDAISM;
and the reprefentations were fuited and
adapted to the peculiar circumftances of
each beholder. The great objects of pagan worfhip were MEN DEIFIED. Paganifm therefore was very fitly reprefented
to Nebuchadnezzar under the form of a
great HUMAN IMAGE, the four metallic
parts of which denoted four empires.
The Jews were ufed to defcribe tyrannical
and perfecuting ftates under the figure of
WILD-BEASTS [16]. The fame empires
are therefore properly fet forth in this vifion by SUCH types ; and the prophet had
the misfortune to fee his own little ftate
defcribed and punifhed under the fame
form. In the beginning of the vifion
" Daniel faw, and, behold! the four winds
of the heaven ftrove upon the great fea,
and FOR GREAT WILD-BEASTS came up"
fucceffively " from the fea, diverfe one
from another." As thefe beafts came out
of a troubled and tempeftuous fea, fo the
empires, reprefented by them, fucceffively
arofe from the ftrivings of the people.
" The

" The FIRST was like a LION." This anfwers to the golden head of the image,
and ftands for the empire of the BABYLO-
NI NS. The Greek and vulgate verfions
read a LIONESS. And Jerome fays exprefsly, that " the Babylonian empire for
its favagenefs and cruelty is not called a
lion but a lionefs; for the writers on natural hiftory report, that the lioneffes are
the fierceft*." If what Jerome here fays
of the fex of the beaft be true, I would
fuppofe, that, at leaft, the head of the
image was female. And thus the two
types would be more properly expreffive
of " Babylon the great, the MOTHER of
harlots and abominations of the earth †."

This lion, or lionefs, at firft " had eagle's
wings, by which it was lifted up from the
earth [17]. But Daniel looked " till the
wings thereof were plucked, and it was
made to ftand upon two feet [18] as a
man, and a man's heart was given to it."
As the foaring of the beaft above the earth
is

* Regnum Babylonium propter fævitiam et crude-
litatem—non LEO fed LEÆNA appellatur. Aiunt enim
hi qui de beftiarum fcripfere naturis, leænas effe fero-
ciores." Hieron. in loc.

† Rev. xvii. 5.

is plainly oppofed to its ftanding upon two feet like a man, with the additional circumftance of " a man's heart being given to it;" the meaning may perhaps be found in that noble EPINIKION, or triumphant ode, upon the fall of Babylon. " How art thou fallen from heaven, O Lucifer, fon of the morning ! How art thou cut down to the ground, which did weaken the nations ! For thou haft faid in thine heart, I will afcend into heaven, I, will exalt my throne above the ftars of God---I will afcend above the heights of the clouds, I will be like the moft high. Yet thou fhalt be brought down to the grave, to the fides of the pit *." If this be the true meaning of the paffage, Daniel lived to fee in reality, what he here faw in vifion, the overthrow of the Babylonian empire.

" The SECOND wild-beaft was like to a BEAR, and it raifed up itfelf on one fide, and it had three ribs in its mouth, betwcen its teeth ; and they faid thus unto it, Arife, devour much flefh." This anfwers to the filver breaft and arms of the image, and reprefents the empire of the MEDES and PERSIANS. " It raifed up itfelf on

D one

* Ifaiah xiv. 12—15.

one fide," for at firft the Medes had the
fuperiority. In this ftate it had only three
ribs, a few bones, between its teeth. But
afterwards it arofe and devoured much
flefh. This is commonly underftood of
the cruelty of the Perfians [19]. But, in
fymbolical language, F L E S H fignifies
R I C H E S, and the oppofition between
three [20] and much, ribs and flefh,
clearly fhews that this empire was to
make larger conquefts, and obtain more
fpoils and riches under the Perfians than
under the Medes. Accordingly we read,
that Xerxes, " the RICHEST of all the
kings of Perfia *, reigned, from India even
unto Ethiopia, over A HUNDRED AND
SEVEN AND TWENTY provinces †.

" The THIRD wild-beaft was like a
LEOPARD, which had upon its back four
wings of a fowl; the wild-beaft had alfo
FOUR HEADS, and dominion was given to
it," to each head. This correfponds with
the belly and thighs of the image, and reprefents the third, or MACEDONIAN, empire under Alexander's fucceffors, for
Alexander himfelf is paffed by. The
term IT, to which dominion was given,

does

does not relate to the beaſt, for the very
ſymbol itſelf implies dominion, but, diſtri-
butively, to the four heads of the beaſt.
We have a ſimilar deſcription of this empire, with its explanation, elſewhere. "A
HE-GOAT came from the weſt---had a notable horn between its eyes --- the great horn
was broken, and for it, " inſtead of it," came
up FOUR notable ones towards the four
winds of heaven.---The rough goat is the
empire of Grecia, and the great horn between
his eyes is the firſt emperor. Now that
being broken, whereas four ſtood up for it,"
inſtead of it, " four kingdoms will ſtand
up out of the nation *." The only difference between the viſions is, that the
goat appeared at firſt with one horn, and
then with four ; whereas the leopard roſe
up at once with its four heads [21]. A
convincing proof, were any proof neceſſary, that Alexander's empire was the ſame
with that of his ſucceſſors.

" The FOURTH wild-beaſt was dreadful
and terrible, and ſtrong exceedingly, and
it had great iron teeth ; it devoured and
brake in pieces and ſtamped the reſidue,"
the remains of the other three, " with its

D 2   feet ;

* Dan. viii. 5—22.

feet; and it was copied [22] from all the
beafts that were before it, and it had TEN
HORNS." This beaft, without a name, anfwers to the iron legs of the image, and
reprefents the ROMAN empire. As Daniel
informs us in general, that this beaft was
copied from the other three, fo St John
has fpecified the feveral parts of this extraordinary compofition. " The wild-beaft
was like unto a LEOPARD, and its feet were
as the feet of a BEAR, and its mouth was
as the mouth of a LION †." The ten
horns of this namelefs beaft anfwer to the
ten toes of the image, and, like them,
fignify the PAGAN provinces of the fourth
empire. It was a moft unhappy conceit
of Mr Collins, to make the ten horns fo
many SUCCESSIVE kings in the KINGDOM,
as he calls it, of the Seleucidæ and Lagidæ.
For though no abfurdity appears in the
notion of ten fucceffive horns, yet the
fancy of ten fucceffive TOES muft bc too
abfurd, even for the head of a freethinker.

Daniel " confidered the horns." He
had difcovered, perhaps, the correfpond-
ence of the fourth beaft with the fourth
part of the image, and of the ten horns
with

---

† Rev. xiii. ?.

with the ten toes. Something, however, was ſtill wanting. He perceived nothing that anſwered to the mountain. He therefore attentively reviewed the ten horns, and obſerved, that " ANOTHER had come up behind them, a LITTLE horn, before whom three [23] of the firſt horns were plucked up." This horn evidently anſwers to the mountain in the former viſion, and conſequently denotes the Jews. There the Jews were conſidered in their ſpiritual capacity, as a CHURCH, and very properly repreſented by a mountain, " the mountain of the Lord's houſe." Here they are ſhewed, in their civil capacity, as a little PROVINCE of the Roman empire, and are as properly repreſented by a horn of the fourth beaſt. It had grown up behind the other ten. It aroſe after them in time, and behind them in place. Thus at the time of the viſion the Jews had no political exiſtence, they were captives in Babylon. And when they returned, and their polity was revived, it was in the remoteſt corner of what was afterwards called the Roman world. We may obſerve farther, that when it is expreſsly

ſaid,

said, " Three horns were plucked up BE-
FORE the little one," it is fairly implied,
that the little-one itself was plucked up
afterwards. The cause of its destruction
follows. " In this horn were eyes like
the eyes of a man, BUT A MOUTH SPEAKING
GREAT, " that is, blasphemous" THINGS."
Our Saviour seems to have had this prophecy in view, when he says to his disci-
ples, " Ye shall hear of wars and rumors
of wars, see that ye be not troubled; for
all these things must come to pass, but the
end is not yet. For nation shall rise against
nation, and kingdom against kingdom,
and there shall be famines, and pestilences,
and earthquakes in divers places. All
these are the BEGINNING of sorrows †."
They are the predicted forerunners of those
unparalleled calamities, which shall not
determine but in the desolations of Jerusalem. " For," as it is added in St Luke,
" these are the days of vengeance, that all
things which are WRITTEN may be FUL-
FILLED ‡."

The prophet continued looking, " till
two thrones were placed" [24] in heaven,
(for

---

† Matt. xxiv. 6—8. Mark xiii. 7, 8.
‡ Luke xxi. 9—22.

(for the prefent fcene is there) " and the antient of days, " the king eternal" did fit" upon one of them, (" his garment was white as fnow, and the hair of his head like the pure wool ; his throne was as the fiery flame, its wheels as burning fire ; a fiery ftream iffued and came forth from before him ; thoufand thoufands minif-tered unto him, and ten thoufand times ten thoufand ftood before him) the judge [25]did fit, and the"prophetic" books were opened." The thrones are here limited to two, becaufe two are fufficient for the purpofe, one of them being placed for the antient of days, and the other for " the fon of man [26]," who will appear pre-fently. The judge is the fame with the antient of days, who is introduced a fe-cond time on account of the defcription in the parenthefis. And I call the books prophetic, becaufe they relate to the com-ing of the TIME when the faints poffeffed the kingdom.

Daniel ftill " beheld, becaufe of the voice of the great words which the horn fpake, till A BEAST was flain, and his BODY de-ftroyed and given to the burning flame. The REST, " the remains," of the beaft, they

had

had their dominion taken away, but their lives were prolonged for a feafon and time." The common fyftem fuppofes, that this was the FOURTH GREAT beaft; whereas it was a FIFTH and a LITTLE one. It was indeed no other than the little horn itfelf now transformed into a beaft. The prophet, who faw the beafts, their fize and number, could not poffibly be under any doubt whether he faw four or five, and whether the fifth was a fmall beaft or a great one. Nor will any unprejudiced reader be under the leaft doubt concerning this matter, if he confiders the whole of the angel's interpretation, and compares one part of it with another. The interpretation has already appeared, and will be given again in its proper place hereafter. In the mean time we may obferve, that the body of this beaft [27] is exprefsly contradiftinguifhed from its other parts, and that, though the body itfelf was deftroyed, the "lives of the remains were prolonged for a feafon and time." That is, the people, reprefented by the beaft, were deftroyed as a body politic; but the lives of the individuals, of thofe who remained [28], were prolonged for an appointed

feafo n

feafon. And, I prefume, I need not to add, that the Jews themfelves bear tefti-' mony to the truth of the prediction.

But this is not all. Though the remains of the beaft had their lives prolonged, yet " their dominion was taken away." What dominion ? The very life of a fymbolical beaft is its dominion. When the beaft therefore is killed, and its body deftroyed, what dominion can be left for its remains ? In anfwer to this queftion I obferve, that the Jews were under a double dominion, TEMPORAL and SPIRITUAL. And as the firft was taken from them by the act of the Romans, fo the latter was taken from them by the act of. God. Jacob himfelf foretold the lofs of this dominion at the very time when he conveyed it to the tribe of Jewdah. " The fcepter [29] fhall not depart from Jewdah, for from him fhall arife the lawgiver until Shiloh," He whofe it is, " fhall come ; but unto him fhall the gathering of the peoples be *." That is, in the words of Shiloh himfelf, " The kingdom of God fhall be taken away from you, and given to a nation bringing forth the fruits of it †."

The

---

* Gen. xlix. 10.   † Matt. xxi. 43.

The FIFTH BEAST being thus deftroyed, Daniel " faw in the night-vifions, and, behold !" the fon of God [30] " like a fon of man, came in the clouds of heaven, and went towards the antient of days, and they brought him near before him. And there was given him dominion, and glory, and a kingdom, that all people, nations, and languages fhould ferve him. His dominion is an everlafting dominion, which fhall not pafs away, and his kingdom that which fhall not be deftroyed." Though Daniel did not underftand, exactly, the meaning of what he had feen, yet he knew enough to alarm and terrify him. He " was grieved in his fpirit in the midft of his body, and the vifions of his head troubled him." He therefore " went near unto one of them that ftood by," (thofe minifters of God which do his pleafure) " and afked the truth of all this," the fignification of the myfteries which he had feen. " So he told me, fays Daniel, and made me know the interpretation of the things."

" Thofe great wild-beafts, namely, thofe four. Four empires fucceffively arife out of the earth. Then the faints of the moft high

high fhall take the kingdom, and poffefs the kingdom for ever, even for ever and ever." Here the myftery begins to open. Four wild-beafts are plainly oppofed to a FIFTH, four GREAT wild-beafts to a SMALL one. That is, four empires are oppofed to a kingdom; the great empires of Babylon, Perfia, Greece, and Rome, to the petty kingdom of Jewdea. The mode of the angel's expreffion is remarkable, and neceffarily leads us to this interpretation. He does not fay, The beafts, or The four beafts, are four empires, (which would have been fufficient if no more than four had appeared) but he fays, " Thofe great beafts, namely, thofe four, are four empires which fucceffively arife out of the earth." He adds, " Then," under the fourth empire, " the faints of the moft high fhall take the kingdom," the kingdom of heaven now forfeited by the Jews, " and fhall poffefs the kingdom for ever and ever."

We, who have the advantage of laying the whole of the angel's interpretation at once before us, and may compare one part of it with another, can readily fee more of his meaning in the general explanation, than Daniel himfelf could poffibly difcover.

It

It will clearly appear hereafter, that the little horn and the beaſt that was ſlain áre one and the ſame kingdom, in different reſpeċts. And both theſe emblems apply with the greateſt exaċtneſs to the Jews. As Jewdea was a Roman province, it was very fitly repreſented by a horn of the fourth beaſt. But though this horn had eyes like the eyes of a man, had the appearance of being humanized, yet he had " a mouth ſpeaking great," that is, blaſphemous " things ;" and he aċted accordingly. No wonder therefore, if his next ſcenical appearance was that of a wild-beaſt, the Jewiſh ſymbol of a tyrannical, perſecuting power. His brother in the Revelation is deſcribed in the ſame language. " I beheld another WILD-BEAST * coming up out of the earth, and he had two horns like the horns of a lamb, but he SPAKE as a DRAGON †."

Daniel, as I have obſerved, could not poſſibly underſtand the full and preciſe meaning of what he had ſeen, nor was his curioſity ſatisfied with the angel's general interpretation. He was therefore deſirous of knowing, more particularly, " the truth of

* Θηρίον.   † Rev. xiii. 11.

of the fourth wild-beaſt, which was co-'
pied from all the others --- and of the ten
horns that were in his head, and of the
other which came up, and before whom
three fell, even of that horn that had eyes"
like the eyes of a man, " and a mouth
that ſpake very great things, whoſe look
was more ſtout than his fellows. I had
looked, ſays the prophet, and the ſame
horn made war with the ſaints, and prevailed againſt them, until the antient of
days came, and judgment was given to the
ſaints of the moſt high, and the time came
that the ſaints poſſeſſed the kingdom."
The angel thus replied.   " The fourth
wild-beaſt.   A fourth empire will be upon
the earth, which will be copied from all"
the preceding " empires, and will devour
the whole earth, and tread it down, and
break it in pieces.   And the ten horns.
Out of this empire ten kings (or kingdoms)
will ariſe, then another will ariſe after
them, and he will be diverſe from the firſt
(ten,) and three kings will be ſubdued,
and he will ſpeak great words againſt the
moſt high, and will wear out the ſaints of
the moſt high, and think to change times
and laws, and they will be given into his
hand

hand until a time and two times and the half of a time. Then the judgment ſhall ſit, and they ſhall take away his dominion, to conſume and to deſtroy it at the end. And the kingdom, and dominion, and the greatneſs of the kingdom under the whole heaven ſhall be given to a people, the ſaints of the moſt high, whoſe kingdom is an everlaſting kingdom, and all dominions ſhall ſerve and obey him."

Here the truth of the interpretation, before given, is fully confirmed. The fourth wild-beaſt is the fourth empire upon earth. The fourth beaſt was a copy of the three preceding ones; and the fourth or Roman empire comprehended the three former, ſo as to be, with its own proper territories, miſtreſs of the whole earth. The ten horns (the number TEN being ſymbolical, and denoting univerſality) are all the PAGAN kingdoms or provinces. The other, which aroſe behind them, is J E W D E A. This horn is not called the eleventh, though it was ſo numerically, but is placed ſingly by itſelf; for, according to Balaam's prediction, " this people were to dwell alone, and not be

reckoned

reckoned among the nations *." " It was DIVERSE from the firſt" horns. And the Jews were diverſe from all other people, particularly in their form of government, which is the very thing intended. It was neither a monarchy, nor a democracy, nor an ariſtocracy, but, as Joſephus properly ſtyles it, a " THEOCRACY" adminiſtered by a deputy ; and this ſingular mode ſubſiſted, throughout the various changes of viſible governors, from MOSES the firſt " king in Jeſhurun" to VESPASIAN the laſt [31]. " And he ſhall ſubdue three kings" or kingdoms, that is, agreeably to the Hebrew idiom [32], three kingdoms ſhall be ſubdued. The fate of theſe kingdoms is deſcribed by no leſs than three different expreſſions †. And, no doubt, the thing itſelf is ſo often repeated, and ſo variouſly expreſsed, that it might take the faſter hold on the attention of the Jews, and be a SIGN to them, when it happened, of their own approaching cataſtrophe. " Ye HYPOCRITES, (ſays our Saviour, in the moſt upbraiding tone, to the Phariſees and Sadducces) ye know how to diſcern the face of the ſky, and can ye not diſcern the

ſigns

---

* Numb. xxiii 9.　　† אתעקרו כפלו יהשפל

figns of the times * ?" and (to the people)
" Ye HYPOCRITES, ye know how to
difcern the face of the fky and of the earth,
but how is it that ye do not difcern this
time § ? " It is plain from this ftrong and
pointed language, that the Jews were poffeffed of fome prophetic figns, which, if
properly attended to, might have led them
to a difcernment of the times. Elfe,
where was the HYPOCRISY in their not dif-
cerning what, in the nature of things, it
was impoffible for them to difcover ? And
if they had, in fact, any fuch prophetic
figns of the times, I know not where to
feek them but in Daniel. The truth is,
that fo far as their, fuppofed, temporal
interefts were concerned, they could and
did fee the prophetic figns. On this occafion their difcernment was fufficiently
quick and penetrating. Puffed up with
the fond and foolifh conceit of a FIFTH
MONARCHY, and of reigning, in their turns,
upon the earth, they overlooked, or ra-
ther they would not difcern, the figns of
their deftruction ; and fo, ftruggling for
the empire, they loft their liberty. " They
thought that the kingdom of God would
                                    imme-

* Matt. xvi. 3.   § Luke xii. 56.

immediately appear +." And, with re-
gard to the time, they thought right, " for
the kingdom of God was among them."
But they would not underftand the true
nature of it, or of its appearance. The
kingdom of God, like God himfelf, is to
be feen only in its effects. " It cometh
not, as our Saviour told them, with obfervation ; neither fhall they fay, Lo here !
or, Lo there ! for, behold ! the kingdom
of God is among you ‖." That is, as we
may interpret the words, The kingdom of
God does not make its appearance, as you
expect, like the Babylonian, Perfian, Macedonian, and Roman, " with a confufed
noife, and garments rolled in blood ;" nor
is it attended with outward pomp and
fplendor. It comes in filence and in peace,
offering itfelf to the hearts and confciences
of men ; it does not appear, though it ex-
ifts, for indeed 'it is already among you,
and you know it not. --- So pure and hea-
venly a kingdom was not fuited to the
tafte and genius of " the children of this
world." It had " no form, nor comelinefs,
nor any beauty, that they fhould defire it."
They therefore rejected the gracious offer

E   of

---

† Luke xix. 11.   ‖ Luke xvii. 20.

of God, and were, in their turn, to be rejected by him. And that they might not
want figns of their approaching deftruction,
they are informed, that three, that is, many
kingdoms, fhall fall and be fubdued before
them. Accordingly, our Saviour repeats
thefe figns to his difciples, exhorts them
" not to be troubled when they heared of
wars, and rumors of wars," for though the
defolations of Jerufalem would certainly,
yet they would not immediately, follow the
conquefts of other nations; and he advifes
them to provide for their own fafety, the
very moment they faw Jerufalem encompaffed with armies (the abomination of
defolation fpoken of by Daniel) by retiring
from Jewdea*. The believing Jews availed themfelves of their mafter's caution,
and were faved [33]. The unbelieving
perifhed with their country.

The reafon of their deftruction is now
more fully difclofed. " He (the king reprefented by the little horn) will fpeak
blafphemous words againft the moft high,
and will wear out the faints of the moft
high, and think to change times and laws,
and they fhall be given into his hand until
a time

* Matt. xxiv. 15, 16. Luke xxi. 20.

a time and two times and the half of a time." Can any one look upon this picture, and not immediately recollect the original, from which it was copied ? Does he not inftantly difcover the powers of Jerufalem crucifying the Chrift, perfecuting the Chriftians, contradicting and blafpheming ? The crucifixion of the Meffiah, though executed by the Romans, is always charged upon the Jews as their own proper act. Jefus himfelf fays to Pilate, " He that delivered me unto thee hath the greater fin †." And St Paul, I prefume, addreffed the high-prieft as the reprefentative of his nation, when he declared, in the fpirit of prophecy, " God will fmite thee, thou whited wall [34]. And doft thou fit to judge me according to the law, yet commandeft me to be fmitten contrary to the law *?" This leads us to the next part of Daniel's prediction. " And he will think to change times and laws." The learned Mr Mede informs us, that " the changing of times and laws is an oriental phrafe to exprefs POTESTATEM αυτοκρατορικην ; " that is, an imperial, felf-derived, and indeed a Godlike power. And did not the Jews affect

E 2   this

---

† John xix. 11.   * Acts xxiii. 3.

this very power, when they oppofed themfelves to Cæfar, to the Mcffiah, and even
to God himfelf? Did they not THINK to
change both the times and the laws? And
did they not perifh in the attempt? Our
bleffed Saviour has given us a very lively
defcription of their conduct, and their fate,
in his parable of " a certain houfholder,
who planted a vineyard, let it out to hufbandmen, and went into a far country for
a long time. And when the time of the
fruit drew near, he fent his fervants to the
hufbandmen, that they might receive the
fruits of it. And the hufbandmen took
his fervants, and beat one, and killed another, and ftoned another. Again he fent
other fervants, more than the firft; and
they did unto them likewife. But laft of
all, he fent unto them his fon, faying,
They will reverence my fon. But when
the hufbandmen faw the fon, they faid
among themfelves, This is the heir, come,
let us kill him, and let us feize on his inheritance. So they caught him, and caft
him out of the vineyard, and flew him.
When the Lord therefore of the vineyard
cometh, what will he do unto thofe hufbandmen? They fay unto him, He will mife-
rably

rably deſtroy thoſe wicked men, and will
let out his vineyard unto other huſbandmen, which will render him the fruits in
their ſeaſons *." The meaning of the parable is ſo eaſy and obvious that even " the
chief prieſts and phariſees perceived it was
ſpoken againſt them." The owner of the
vineyard is God, the vineyard is his church
or kingdom, and the huſbandmen are the
Jews. The ſervants are the prophets, from
Moſes to the baptiſt, all of whom were
perſecuted, and ſome murdered [35]. The
ſon is the Meſſiah, the Son of God, whom
the Jews ſlew in hopes of poſſeſſing his
kingdom. You know the event. The
kingdom was taken from them, and tranſ-
lated to the Gentiles. And, as we learn
from Joſephus, the Jewiſh war laſted about
three years and a half [36]. So that the
ſaints, or Chriſtians, were given into the
hands of the Jews " UNTIL a time and two
times and the half of a time."

Theſe are the two laſt events foretold by
Daniel. " Then," at the end of thoſe three
years and a half, " the judgement ſhall ſit,
and they ſhall take away his dominion, the
dominion of the little horn, to conſume and
to deſtroy it at the end. And the kingdom

* Matt. xxi. 3—41.

and dominion and the greatnefs of the
kingdom under the whole heaven fhall be
given to a people, the faints of the moft
high, whofe kingdom is an everlafting
kingdom, and all dominions fhall ferve
and obey him." It now appears very
plainly, that the little horn and the beaft,
which were deftroyed, are one and the
fame kingdom in different refpects. Confequently, this beaft cannot be the fourth,
the reprefentative of the Roman empire.
For though the fame thing or perfon may,
in different refpects, be reprefented in the
fame vifion by different fymbols [37], and
therefore the fame kingdom may be here
reprefented both by a horn and by a beaft,
yet the fame empire cannot poffibly be ty-
pified by the horn of a beaft and by the
beaft itfelf. Becaufe this is the very fame
contradiction as to call a member the body,
or a part of any thing the whole of it. It
is a contradiction in ideas, as well as in
terms. Befides, the little horn in this vifion anfwers to the firft mountain in the
other. Now the mountain cannot poffibly
fignify any other kingdom than that of
the Jews, in a certain refpect. And therefore, " if ye will receive it," the little horn

or

or beaft muft neceffarily fignify the fame kingdom in another.

The Jewifh kingdom was deftroyed by the Romans, who had no other intentions, at firft, than to chaftife a rebellious people. But providence generally brings about its own purpofes by means of fecond caufes. And as the Romans were the inftruments of the Jews in the crucifixion of Chrift, fo they were now employed as the inftruments of providence in the deftruction of the Jews ; their apoftafy from the Romans naturally bringing on the allotted punifhment of their apoftafy from God. " The judge was feated on his throne in heaven, and their dominion was taken away." " Three horns fell before the little one,"' and other rebellious provinces were fubdued by the Romans before the Jews *. But thofe horns only fell, thofe provinces were only humbled ; they fubmitted, and were fpared. " The little horn fell "--- never to rife again ; the Jews perfifted in their oppofition, to God and to

E 4 Cæfar,

---

* Proximus annus civili bello intentus, quantum ad JUDÆOS per otium tranfiit. Pace per ITALIAM parta, & EXTERNÆ cu æ redicre. Augebat iras, quod SOLI JUDÆI NON CESSISSENT. Taciti Hiftoriar. lib. v. 19.

Cæfar, and perifhed. Their perdition was exhibited to the prophet by that of " a wild-beaft, whofe BODY was given to a burning flame." Our bleffed Saviour, if I miftake not, clearly alludes to this paffage, when he fays to the difciples, " Wherefo- ever the BODY is, thither will the EAGLES be gathered together †." The expreffion is indeed proverbial, and may, no doubt, be applied generally to the deftruction of one army by another [39]. But as no true critic will venture to deny, that the term " eagles" has, in this application, a direct reference to the Roman eagles, fo I will conclude, for myfelf, that the term " body" has the fame reference to the body of the Jewifh beaft, whofe dominion was to be taken away, and deftroyed, at the end.

The end, here fpoken of, is that of the " three times and a half," the continuance of the Jewifh war with the Romans. " Then, fays the angel, there fhall be an END of the matter," a period fhall be put to the Jewifh nation and polity. Our Saviour fore- tells the fame thing. Having mentioned va- rious events that were to precede the de- ftruction of Jerufalem, he adds, " Then fhall

† Luke xvii. 37.

ſhall the END come *," the end of the Moſaic church and ſtate. And have not theſe
predictions received the moſt exact completion ?

Daniel was a patriot, as well as a prophet. It is therefore no wonder, that he
was ſo deeply affected with this tremend-
ous ſcene. " His cogitations much troubled him, and his countenance changed in
him." And the bleſſed Jeſus too, who
was more than patriot, could not refrain
from tears, when he ſaw the approaching
fate of his unhappy country. " He beheld the city, ſays the evangeliſt, and wept
over it †." Daniel " kept the matter in
his heart." And every other Jew will do
well to lay this matter to heart, to conſi-
der, with candor, ſerioufneſs, and attention, the many ſtriking particulars recorded by this prophetic evangeliſt, and recorded with the ſame preciſion and accuracy,
as if he had lived and written after the
events. What rational account can the
Jews pretend to give of the deſtruction of
their city and temple, and of the continued
deſolations of their country ? The Romans
" could have had no power at all againſt
them,

them, except it had been given to them from above." What then was the opprobrious crime, which brought down fo fignal a calamity upon this once highly favoured people? Let them look into the writings of their own prophet Daniel, and there they may read their crime in that of the HORN, and their punifhment in that of the BEAST. " The horn fpake blafphemous words againft the moft high;" and the Jews refufed to fubmit to the government of God, in the way which he had appointed. " If thou let this man go, faid the Jews to Pilate, thou art not Cæfar's friend. Whofoever maketh himfelf a king fpeaketh againft Cæfar ‡." And again, " We have no king but Cæfar †." God took them at their word, and their king was their deftruction.

The deftruction of Jerufalem made way for the advancement of the kingdom of God; or, in other words, the abolition of the Jewifh theocracy upon earth, made way for the eftablifhment of the Meffiah's kingdom in heaven, and was indeed a proof of it. Our Saviour exprefly appeals to it as fuch. " Immediately after the tribulation

‡ John xix. 12.   † John xix. 15.

tion of thofe days fhall the fun be darken-
ed, and the moon fhall not give her light,
and the ftars fhall fall from heaven, and
the powers of the heaven fhall be fhaken."
Some may poffibly imagine this prophecy
to be a defcription of the falling world, in
the literal fenfe of the terms. But our Saviour intends nothing more than a ceffa-
tion of the Jewifh polity, expreffed in fymbolic language. He adds, " And then fhall
appear the fign of THE SON OF MAN IN
HEAVEN ||. Well might he call this the
fign of the fon of man's being in heaven,
when the angel had fo long before made
the overthrow of Jerufalem the immediate
forerunner of the fon of man's inthroniza-
tion into his kingdom in heaven. " When-
ever the theocracy was abrogated, it muft
needs be done, fays a great writer, in the
fame folemn manner in which it was efta-
blifhed. --- Nor, indeed, could it have been
abolifhed without diffolving the whole
frame of the republic ; fince all the laws
of it, whether as to their equity, force, or
fitnefs, as well as the whole ritual of worfhip, refpected and referred to God as civil
governor ‡." ·Take then a piece of hiftory
from

|| Matt. xxiv. 29.   ‡ Div. Leg. vol. iv. p. 243.

from a Roman writer, no ways interested
in the dispute between Jews and Christians.
Speaking of the PRODIGIES (or SIGNS)
which happened during the Jewish war,
my author mentions this among the rest.
" Expassæ subito DELUBRI fores, & audita
major humanâ vox, EXCEDERE DEOS, simul
ingens motus EXCEDENTIUM *." It is im-
possible, I believe, to express the ABOLI-
TION of the THEOCRACY in clearer or in
stronger terms.

The Jewish theocracy, that " wall of
partition," being thus removed, the Messiah's kingdom was extended over all nations. " There was given him dominion,
and glory, and a kingdom, that ALL people, nations, and languages, (represented
by the SEVEN remaining horns) should
serve him. His dominion is an everlasting
dominion, which shall not pass away, and
his kingdom that which shall not be destroyed." This is elsewhere called the
kingdom of the saints. " The kingdom,
and dominion, and the greatness of the
kingdom under the whole heaven shall be
given to a people, the SAINTS of the most
high, whose kingdom is an everlasting
kingdom,

* Taciti Historiar. lib. v. 13.

kingdom, and all dominions [throughout
the Roman empire] fhall ferve and obey
him." The Jews were once the peculiar
people of God, and, from their relation to
him, diftinguifhed by the honourable ap-
pellation of faints. " Gather my SAINTS
together unto me, fays God by the pfalm-
ift, thofe that have made a covenant with
me with facrifice∗." And fo they are called throughout the Old Teftament, and
even in Daniel too †. But when they oppofed and blafphemed God and his Chrift,
then the ftyle is changed, they are exhibited among " the BEASTS of the people" by
the fame opprobrious fymbol, and the glo-
rious character of SAINTS is transferred to
the Chriftians. Hence St Paul, fpeaking
of himfelf before his converfion as a limb
of Antichrift, informs Agrippa, that"many
of the SAINTS he had fhut up in prifon,
having received authority from the chief
priefts §." Hence too he addreffes his epiftles " to the SAINTS --- at Rome, Corinth,
Ephefus, Philippi, and Coloffe." This is
not a partial diftinction of fome Chriftians
from the reft (as fanatics, of all denomi-
nations, are too apt to appropriate the character

* Pfal. l. 5. † Dan. viii. 24. § Acts xxvi. 10.

racter to themselves) but it is the common
title of the whole family, under their covenanted relation to God and his Son, and
includes " every faint in Chrift Jefus *,"
in oppofition both to Jews and Gentiles ;
and particularly to the former, the one
fcripture ANTICHRIST. And here, perhaps, it may not be improper to obferve,
that the term " Antichrift" does not always
denote a perfon, but fometimes a kingdom
--- the kingdom of SATAN oppofing and
claiming to be the kingdom of God [40].
It is the proper character of thofe "LIARS
who fay that they are JEWS, and are not, but
are the fynagogue of Satan [41]." Thus
the Babylonian KING ftands for the Babylonian KINGDOM †, and the term CHRIST
fignifies the Chriftian CHURCH ‡. In like
manner the Jewifh PONTIF may be ftyled,
reprefentatively, ANTICHRIST. And I
fcruple not to call the Latin PONTIF, as the
head and reprefentative of his church, by
the fame title, for he evidently bears upon
his crown the NUMBER of the NAME of the
apocalyptic BEAST [42]. And thus the
tranfition from one antichrift to the other
is

* Phil. iv. 21.   † Dan. ii. 38.
‡ 1 Cor. xii. 12.

is eaſy and natural, each of them being to be found within the pale of the church.

I will ſhut up my remarks on this prophecy with an application to the members of the papal communion, and to ourſelves.

The church of ROME is, in the opinion of its votaries, the only TRUE church of Chriſt; and one of the boaſted NOTES or MARKS of its truth is VISIBILITY, founded in TEMPORAL power and dominion. Now, ſuppoſing VISIBILITY to be a proper MARK of " the kingdom that cometh NOT WITH OBSERVATION, and allowing TEMPORAL authority to be a diſtinguiſhing NOTE of " the kingdom that is NOT OF THIS WORLD," yet it may be obſerved, that a TRUE church may, in length of time, degenerate into a FALSE one. The JEWS were, once, the peculiar people of God, and their church was the only TRUE one. It was originally founded by God himſelf on TEMPORAL promiſes, had a viſible, magnificent TEMPLE, and a rich, luxurious, politic PRIESTHOOD. In ſhort, it had every advantage and privilege that even a cardinal can eſteem eſſential to a true church. And yet, with all theſe outward privileges and advantages, it fell ---- firſt into apoſtaſy, and

and afterwards into perdition. This then should be a conftant memento to the papal church, " that thinketh it ftandeth, to take heed left it fall." This is not my ob--fervation but St Paul's. Comparing the Jewifh church to a good olive tree, and the Gentiles to a wild one, he reafons with the latter in the following remarkable words. " If fome of the branches be broken off, and thou, being a wild olive tree, wert grafted in amongft them, and with them partakeft of the root and fatnefs of the olive tree, boaft not againft the branches. But if thou boaft, thou beareft not the root, but the root thee. Thou wilt fay then, The branches were broken off, that I might be grafted in. Well, be it fo; becaufe of unbelief they were broken off, and thou ftandeft by faith. Be not high-minded, but fear. For if God fpared not the natural branches, he will by no means fpare thee. Behold therefore the goodnefs and the feverity of God; on them which fell, feverity; but towards thee good-nefs, IF THOU CONTINUE in his goodnefs : OTHERWISE, THOU ALSO---(the apoftle is addreffing the church of ROME --- THOU ALSO) SHALT BE CUT OFF * [43]."

" COME

* Rom. xi. 17—22.

" COME OUT OF HER, therefore, MY PEOPLE,

THAT YE BE NOT PARTAKERS OF HER SINS,

AND THAT YE RECEIVE NOT OF HER PLAGUES *."

WE indeed have, prudiſhly, withdrawn ourſelves from the groſser pollutions of that meretricious community.   How far a ſecond REFORMATION may be either neceſſary or expedient, I muſt not take upon me to determine. This, however, may be ſaid with truth, and therefore, it is hoped, without offence---That the more there is " OF THIS WORLD" in our ecclefiaſtical eftabliſhment, the nearer it is to POPERY, and the farther from the SIMPLICITY OF THE GOSPEL.

* Rev. xviii. 4.

F   THE

THE
FALL of JEWDAISM,
IN THE
REIGN of VESPASIAN.

Gabriel's Prophecy.

SEVENTY WEEKS are determined for thy PEOPLE, and for thy HOLY CITY, TO DESTROY THE WICKED ONE, and to fill up fins, to make reconciliation for iniquity, and to bring in everlafting juftification, and to feal up prophetic vifion, and TO ANOINT THE MOST HOLY ONE:

Know therefore and underftand.

From the promulgation of a commandment to REBUILD Jerufalem UNTO Meffiah the prince, fhall be SEVEN weeks and SIXTY-TWO weeks.

IT SHALL BE REBUILT, the ftreet and the furrow, even in the LITTLE of the times. In the latter part of the SIXTY-

TWO

TWO weeks MESSIAH WILL BE CUT OFF, for they will not be his.

Wherefore the people of the prince that fhall come fhall overthrow the city and the fanctuary, and the end thereof fhall be with a flood; and at the end of the war defolations are determined.

And he fhall caufe a covenant to prevail with ALL [nations.]

[And] in ONE week, even in HALF of the week, he fhall caufe the facrifice and the oblation to ceafe; for with a wing [an army] of abominations he fhall caufe defolations, even until the confummation, and that determined fhall be poured upon the defolators.

DANIEL ix. 1---27.

In the former prediction the FALL of Jewdaifm is folemnly announced, in this the TIME of it. " SEVENTY WEEKS are " determined for thy PEOPLE, and for thy " HOLY CITY." This, you fee, is the ut- moft fpace of time allotted, in the dec.ees of heaven, for the exiftence of the city and people of Jerufalem. Within that period all the circumftances foretold fhall come to pafs. The fcene opens with the reftora-

tion of Jerufalem, and clofes with her deftruction.

The Jews had weeks of YEARS as well
as of DAYS. And thefe SEVENTY WEEKS,
during which the JEWS were to be a PEO-
PLE and JERUSALEM a CITY, have a plain
reference to the SEVENTY YEARS of its DE-
SOLATIONS. Mofes himfelf, among other
threatenings, denounced the following.
"Your LAND SHALL BE DESOLATE, and
" your cities wafte. Then fhall the land en-
" joy her SABBATHS as long as it lieth DESO-
" LATE, and ye be in your enemies land;
" even then fhall the land reft, and enjoy
" her fabbaths. As long as it lieth DESO-
" LATE, it fhall reft, becaufe it did not reft
" in your SABBATHS when ye dwelt upon
" it *."   Accordingly, when the fins of
the Jews were ripe for this vengeance, Jeremiah foretold, that "the whole land fhould
be a DESOLATION --- SEVENTY YEARS †,"
the number of SABBATHS which the Jews
had neglected to obferve when they dwelt
upon the land ‡. Daniel therefore, foon
after

* Lev. xxvi. 33—35.   † Jer. xxv. 11.

‡ " He brought upon them the king of the Chaldees,
" who carried them away to Babylon, where they were
" fervants to him and his fons," and, " until the reign
of

after the overthrow of the BABYLONIAN empire, and fome few years before the reign of PERSIA, reflecting upon the prophetic denunciations of Mofes and Jeremiah, applies himfelf, in the moft pathe-tic ftrains of prayer and fupplication, to the Lord God, befeeching him to " turn " away his anger and his fury from his " city Jerufalem, his holy mountain, and " to caufe his face to fhine upon his defo-" late fanctuary, for the Lord" Meffiah's " fake [44]." His prayer was heared. " At the beginning of his fupplication a " commandment came forth," and the angel Gabriel was fent to inform him, that feventy weeks were allotted for the exiftence of his people and holy city. As if he had faid, the prefent defolations of Jerufalem are fixed for SEVENTY, or TEN TIMES SEVEN years; but from the reftoration of Jerufalem to her future defolations fhall be SEVENTY TIMES SEVEN.

The things in general to be brought about within the compafs of the weeks are

F 3 th:fe.

" of the kingdom of PERSIA, to fulfil the word of the " Lord by the mouth of Jeremiah, until the land had " enjoyed her SABBATHS, "for " as long as fhe was defo " late fhe kept fabbath, to fulfil THREESCORE AND TEN " years." 2 Chron. xxxvi 11——21.

thefe. "To destroy THE wicked one*."
This is no other (in the primary fenfe of
the term) than the " LITTLE HORN" and
fifth " BEAST " exhibited in the foregoing
vifion, " that man of fin, the fon of per-
" dition, THAT wicked one, whom the
" Lord fhall confume with the fpirit of his
" mouth, and deftroy with the brightnefs
" of his coming [45] ‡."

    " To fill up fins."   Here are two read-
ings, occafioned by the fimilitude of two
letters in the original ||.   But, take which
of them you pleafe, the fenfe is the fame ;
" to fill up fins."   And at the time foretold the fins of the Jewifh nation were at
their height.   "FILL YE UP then the mea-
fure of your fathers §," faid Jefus to the
unbelieving Pharifees.   Accordingly they
proceeded " to fill it up" in a few days after
by crucifying the Lord of life.   Hence St
Paul defcribes them as perfons who both
killed the Lord Jefus, and their own prophets, and perfecuted the apoftles ; as dif-
pleafing to God, and contrary to all men,
" FILLING UP THEIR SINS †."

                                        " To

* הבשע   ‡ 2 Theff. ii. 3—8.
‖ להתם לדתם   § Matt. xxiii. 32.
† 1 Theff. ii. 15, 16.

" To make reconciliation for iniquity."
This is fo diftinguifhing a part in the character of MESSIAH, that he is ftyled, by
the antient Jews, איש כפר " the man of pro-
" pitiation, " or " the atonement-maker."
Ifaiah had long before defcribed him as " a
" lamb brought to the flaughter, making
" his life an offering for fin, and bearing
" the iniquities of all *." And who has
looked into the gofpel, and has not there
beholden " JESUS, THE LAMB OF GOD, THE
" PROPITIATION for the fins of the
" world ?"

Juftification is the confequence of atone-
ment. It therefore immediately follows
---" and to bring in everlafting righteouf-
" nefs" or juftification. " Be it known
" unto you, Men and Brethren" (fays the
apoftle, in his fpirited addrefs to the Jews
at Antioch) " that through this" Jefus
" is preached unto you the forgivenefs of
" fins, and by him all that believe are juf-
" tified from all things †." The angel
ftyles this juftification " everlafting," or the
juftification " of ages," in oppofition to
legal juftification, which was only tempo-
rary, and confined to the Jewifh age.

E 4   Whereas

---

* Ifaiah. liii. 7—12.   † Acts xiii. 38, 39.

Whereas the juſtification to be brought in by the death and reſurrection of Meſ-ſiah is, in the ſtricteſt ſenſe, everlaſting; being intended for the benefit of all ages, and being itſelf, like its divine author, " the ſame yeſterday, and to day, and for " ever." Hence the blood of Jeſus, " the " Lamb ſlain from the foundation of the " world," is called " the blood of the ever-" laſting covenant* ." And in this ſenſe we are to underſtand that remarkable ex-preſſion in the ſame epiſtle; where St Paul, oppoſing the ſacrifice of Jeſus to the legal oblations, ſays, " If the blood of bulls and " of goats ſanctifieth to the purifying of " the fleſh, how much more ſhall the " blood of Chriſt, who δια πνυματ Θ αιωνιον" (not thro' THE eternal Spirit, meaning his own divinity or the holy ghoſt, but) " with " AN ETERNAL SPIRIT[46]," power or efficacy, " offered himſelf without ſpot to " God, purge your conſcience from dead " works † ?"

" To ſeal up viſion and prophecy," that is, prophetic viſion. Viſion and prophecy are here ſaid to be " ſealed" in the days of Meſſiah, becauſe in him they were to re-ceive

ceive their completion. The Jews themfelves underftand the words in this fenfe.
" All the prophecies fhall be fulfilled at
" the coming of Meffiah." Now he
who claimed the Meffiahfhip declared, that
he " came to fulfil the law and the prophets *. "And whoever impartially confiders
the feveral types and prophecies relating to
Messiah, will find that they all meet in
Jesus, by a wonderful coincidence, like
different rays in the fame center.

" And to anoint the moft holy." The
perfon who delivered this prophecy concerning Meffiah was the angel Gabriel.
And the fame divine meffenger, when he
was predicting the birth of Jefus to his
virgin mother, expreffly ftyles him " the
" holy one," and fays," He fhall be great,
" and fhall be called the fon of the High-
" eft, and the Lord God fhall give unto
" him the" fpiritual " throne of his father
" David; and he fhall reign over the
" houfe of Jacob for ever, and of his king-
" dom there fhall be no end †."

The angel now goes on to inform us of
the time and manner in which thefe great
events

---

* Matt. v. 17.   † Luke i. 32—35.

events are to be accomplifhed. " Know " therefore and underftand.

" From the promulgation of A com- " mandment to rebuild [47] Jerufalem " unto Meffiah the prince fhall be feven " weeks and fixty two weeks." The com- mencement of thefe weeks is the great point in difpute. Various are the affertions, ar- guments, demonftrations of the celebrated writers upon the fubject. Where then fhall we fix? Or what is that precife point of time marked out by the prophecy? Now, with leave of the chronologers, the refolu- tion of the queftion is not very difficult. For, as one of the beft of them confeffes, " This prophecy expreffeth the time that was determined upon the people of Daniel, that is the Jews, and upon the holy city, that is Jerufalem, the whole of which was feventy weeks *." The learned connector has indeed a figurative interpretation, and he fays, that " all was accom- plifhed at the death of Chrift." But I will fo far prefume upon the privilege of com- mon fenfe, as to fuppofe, that the Jews ceafed not to be a people, nor Jerufalem to be a city, till the reign of Vefpafian.

" The

---

* Prideaux Connect. Vol. I. p. 262,3. 8vo.

" The end of the weeks" (to borrow the Doctor's method of reafoning, which is very fimple, and ftrictly logical) " being thus fixed, it doth neceffarily determine us where to place the beginning of them, that is four hundred and ninety years before."

Reckon then from the DESTRUCTION OF JERUSALEM in the SECOND year of VESPA-SIAN to the SECOND year of DARIUS NOTHUS, and you will find the number of years, according to Ptolemy's canon, [48]FOUR HUNDRED AND NINETY, or there-abouts, for exactnefs of computation is not in this cafe to be expected, and perhaps is hardly poffible. And the fcriptures, fairly and candidly interpreted, place THE COMMANDMENT TO REBUILD THE TEM-PLE, the principal part of JERUSALEM, the very part from which it received its diftin-guifhing denomination of the HOLY CITY, in the SECOND year of the fame DARIUS.

Ezra informs us, that " when the adver-faries of Jewdah heared that the children of the captivity builded the temple to the Lord God of Ifrael, they weakened the hands of the people of Jewdah, and troubled them in building, and hired counfellors againft them, to fruftrate their purpofe, all the

days

days of Cyrus king of Perſia, and until"
and during "the reign of Darius" Hysta-
spis " king of Perſia. And in the reign of
Ahasuerus, Xerxes [49] in the beginning
of his reign, wrote they unto him an accuſation againſt the inhabitants of Jewdah and
Jeruſalem. And in the days of Artaxerxes" Longimanus " wrote they unto the
king, who gave a commandment to cauſe the
work to ceaſe. Then they went up in haſte
to Jeruſalem unto the Jews, and made
them ceaſe by force and power. So it
ceaſed unto the second year of Darius"
Nothus " king of Perſia *. Then the
elders of the Jews builded, and they proſpered through the propheſying of Haggai
and Zechariah; and they builded and finiſhed it according to the commandment of
Cyrus and Darius" Nothus, " and Artaxerxes" Mnemon " king of Perſia §."
The account then plainly ſtands thus.
Cyrus favored the Jews with a decree to
rebuild their temple, and ordered an allow-
ance out of the treaſury towards defraying
the expences ‡. But the Samaritans, who
were enemies to the work, corrupted the
officers in the Perſian court, and ſo prevailed

* Ch. iv. 1—24.   § Ch. vi. 14.   ‡ Ch. vi. 4.

ed with their bribes, that the royal bounty was ftopped during the reigns of CYRUS, CAMBYSES, SMERDIS the ufurper, and DARIUS Hyftafpis. A method, which ferved " to fruftrate the purpofe" of the indigent Jews as effectually, as if the kings themfelves had iffued out their imperial prohibitions.

When AHASUERUS, or XERXES, came to the throne, the Samaritans changed their fyftem, and, inftead of bribing the officers, they addreffed the king himfelf, " and wrote an accufation againft the inhabitants of Jewdah and Jerufalem." What the articles of this accufation were, and what effect it produced, we know not. The hiftorian only remarks, that it was fent " in the beginning of the reign" of Ahafuerus. It is therefore probable, that this accufation gave way to that more important one of " Haman *" againft the whole body of the Jews. Here indeed, through the interpofition of the queen ‡, who was a Jewefs, they triumphed, and had their full revenge of their enemies. This, one would think, was the proper feafon for profecuting the work

* Efther iii. 8, 9.
‡ Ham-Eftris, called fimply, in fcripture, Efther.

work of the houſe of the Lord. But, I know not how, the Jews were ever moſt wanting to their duty in the days of their proſperity.

In the time of ARTAXERXES Longimanus we find an accuſation at large from the Samaritans, together with the king's decree againſt the building, which was executed with the utmoſt rigor. " Then ceaſed the work of the houſe of God which is at Jeruſalem. So it ceaſed unto the SECOND year of DARIUS" Nothus " king of Perſia." That is, it then ceaſed by FORCE, as it had before ceaſed by STRATAGEM, unto the reign of Nothus.

But now the time is come when JERUSALEM, THE HOLY CITY, MUST BE BUILT. The accompliſhment of prophecy depends upon it. No wonder therefore, if you find God himſelf commanding and incouraging the work, defeating the Samaritans, animating the Jews, and inclining the hearts of the kings of Perſia to protect and aſſiſt them. " They builded, and proſpered through the propheſying of Haggai and Zechariah ; and they builded and finiſhed it according to the commandment of the God of Iſrael, and according to the commandment of CYRUS, and DARIUS" Nothus, and

" and ARTAXERXES" Mnemon " king of
Perfia." The houfe indeed, that is, the
mere building, was finifhed in the fixth
year of Darius " Nothus," and the feaft of
dedication was kept with great joy *. But
the ornamental part, " the beautifying of ·
the houfe of the Lord +," as Ezra expreffes it, was not finifhed till the time of Artaxerxes Mnemon; in the feventh year of
whofe reign a decree was granted to EZRA
for that purpofe ‡. And in the twentieth of
the fame Artaxerxes a new decree was granted to NEHEMIAH to complete the other build-
ings of the city, which he accomplifhed in
twelve years §. Thùs the firft divifion of
the angel's prophecy was fulfilled. " From
the promulgation of a commandment TO
REBUILD JERUSALEM unto Mefliah the
prince fhall be SEVEN WEEKS and fixty two
weeks; IT SHALL BE REBUILT, the ftreet
and the wall, even in the LITTLE of thofe
times." For from the fecond year of Darius Nothus, which was the year of Nabonaffar 327, to the thirty fecond of Artaxerxes Mnemon, the year of Nabonaffar
376,

---

* Ezra vi. 15, 16.   † Ezra vii. 27. ‡ ver. 23.
§ Compare Nehem. v. 14. vii. 4. xi. 1.

376, are juſt " ſeven weeks" of years according to Ptolemy's canon ‖.

Thoſe reſpectable writers, Joſeph Scaliger and Joſeph Mede, fixed the commencement of the weeks where I have placed it. Others, however, no leſs reſpectable *, have urged an objection to it from the prophet Haggai. " Who is left among you that ſaw this houſe in its firſt glory ? And how do ye ſee it now ? Is it not in your eyes in compariſon of it as nothing †?" " This text, they ſay, plainly expreſſes, that ſome were then alive who had ſeen the firſt temple, and were capable of comparing it with the ſecond. And therefore if this Darius were Darius Nothus, they muſt have been of an age BEYOND BELIEF. From the deſtruction of the temple to the ſecond of Darius I. were only SIXTY EIGHT years. From the deſtruction of the temple to the ſecond of Darius II were an HUNDRED AND SIXTY SIX years. And where PROBABILITY and IMPROBABILITY appear ſo plainly upon the face of the different calculations, they think the diſtance of time may be admitted as a ſufficient argument to determine the queſtion."

To

‖ Thus, 326+49=376.   * See Sir Iſaac Newton,
Dean Prideaux, &c.   † Hag. iii. 3.

To which I anſwer in the words of a very illuſtrious writer, on another occaſi- on. " The Promiſes of God have never " borrowed help from MORAL PROBA- " BILITIES. His promiſes to ABRAHAM " were not of this kind *." And why then ſhould they be of this kind to the Children of Abraham ? The Jews lived under an ex- traordinary diſpenſation of providence. LONG LIFE was the general promiſe of the Moſaic law to the obedient. And this promiſe was particularly repeated at the time we are ſpeaking of. " There ſhall yet OLD men and OLD women dwell in the ſtreets of Jeruſalem, and every man with his ſtaff in his hand for VERY AGE †." Who now can think it improbable, when events correſpond ſo exactly with every part of the propheſy, that ſome among the Jews ſhould be found of an exceeding great Age ? " IF IT BE MARVELLOUS IN THE EYES OF THE PEOPLE IN THESE DAYS, SHOULD IT ALSO BE MARVELLOUS IN MINE EYES, SAITH THE LORD OF HOSTS ‖[50] ?" I obſerve farther, that our Saviour him-

G ſelf

---

* Biſhop Sherlock's ſermons, Vol. I. P. 222.
† Zech. viii. 4.   ‖ Ibid. 6.

self, one of the best interpreters of scrip-
ture, has placed the end of the weeks, and
by necessary consequence their beginning,
where we place it. "When ye shall see
Jerusalem compassed with armies---the
abomination of desolation spoken of by
Daniel the prophet---then know that the
desolation thereof is nigh *." Here the
end of Jerusalem and the end of the weeks
are plainly contemporary. Our Saviour,
as well as Daniel, places " the abomination of desolation" in the last week. The
first week therefore must commence from
the second year of Darius Nothus, four
hundred and ninety years before. This
deserves the serious consideration of believ-
ers [51]. Nor can unbelievers, without
the greatest absurdity, object to our Saviour's
authority in the present instance; his comment being at once a proof of Daniel's in-
spiration and of his own Messiahship. For
the case stands thus. Daniel foretold certain things to be accomplished, within a
given period, by Messiah. Jesus foretells
the same things, and applies them to himself. The event answered to the predictions. Consequently, Daniel was a true

pro-

* Matt. xxiv. 15. Luke xxi. 20.

prophet, and Jefus is the Meffiah foretold by Daniel.

The fum of what has been faid is this. ---The Angel declares, that FROM the promulgation of a commandment to rebuild Jerufalem TO its final deftruction, fhall be SEVENTY WEEKS, or four hundred and ninety years. A commandment to build Jerufalem was promulged in the fecond year of the reign of DARIUS. According to the fcripture account of the Perfian kings, this Darius was the SECOND of that name. The fecond Darius in the canon of Ptolemy is NOTHUS. From the fecond year of DARIUS NOTHUS to the deftruction of Jerufalem in the fecond of VESPASIAN were SEVENTY WEEKS, or four hundred and ninety years. If thefe principles are allowed, and they cannot reafonably be difputed, the confequence is inevitable, That, as the weeks END in the fecond year of VESPASIAN, they muft neceffarily BEGIN in the fecond of DARIUS NOTHUS.

Having thus fettled the commencement of the weeks, we may now proceed to explain and to apply the remaining parts of the prophefy.

" From the promulgation of a com-

mand-

mandment" in the fecond year of Darius Nothus " to rebuild Jerufalem, unto MESSIAH THE PRINCE, fhall be SEVEN weeks and SIXTY TWO weeks." Our blefsed Saviour was a PROPHET a PRIEST and a KING; and therefore he was in each of thefe refpects the MESSIAH. But the Angel points at him in his regal character. " Unto Mefliah the PRINCE." This is the character, by this he ftands eminently diftinguifhed in the writings of the Jews. " King Mefliah" is the conftant defcription of him who was to redeem Ifrael. Now it is obfervable, that, though the promifes of this king are fo frequent in the fcriptures of the old teftament, he is no where abfolutely ftyled Mefliah but in the prophefy before us *. This is a demonftrative proof

of

* " Abfque hoc loco, vix unum vet. teft. affignare poffis, quo niteretur ifta expectatio MESSIÆ, h. e. principis EO NOMINE infigniti. De UNCTIONE alibi legimus, et aliquando de UNCTO DOMINI, fed nufquam alibi, quod memini, de MESSIA abfolute, ut loquuntur, pofito; et tamen apud Judæos nomen hoc de PRINCIPE VENTURO celeberrimum erat. Joh. i. 41. inquit Andreas Petro, " invenimus MESSIAM;" imo etiam apud Samaritanos obtinuit. Joh. iv. 25. " Scio quod MESSIAS veniet." Unde vero hoc nomen adeo percrebuit, nifi ex hoc præclaro vaticinio? Buxtorffius (Lexic.
Rabbin.

of the undoubted Jewiſh application of this propheſy to their Meſſiah. And thus we diſcover the true reaſon why this title in particular was ſo generally given by the Jews, in the age of Jeſus, to their expected deliverer. For what could be more natural, at the very TIME MARKED OUT, as they ſuppoſed, by Daniel for expecting his appearance, than to call him by the very ſame NAME and TITLE attributed to him by Daniel? The time here fixed for his COMING, in his regal capacity, is the ſeventieth or laſt week; for the term of ſixty nine weeks was to be run out before he came. " UNTO Meſſiah the prince ſhall be SEVEN weeks and SIXTY TWO weeks." And he came accordingly ; firſt to diſſolve the polity of the JEWS, and then " to take the HEATHEN for his inheritance, and the utmoſt parts of the earth for his poſſeſſion."

The angel having mentioned two periods, a little period of " ſeven weeks," and a large period of " ſixty two," he immediate-

G 3   ly

v. Meſſiah) enumerat LXX plus minus locos, in quibus nomen MESSIÆ occurrit in paraphraſi Chaldaica ; inde conſtat maximo apud Judæos confenſu illud principi ſuo convenire, quem ardentibus votis præſtolabantur." Epiſtola cl. Stillingſlect ad I. Marſham.

ly tells the prophet what was to be done
in each of them. " In the LITTLE of the
times it," Jerusalem, " shall be rebuilt, the
street and the furrow ;" that is, Jerusalem
shall be built again within and without,
there shall be not only a temple for the God
and king of Israel, but houses also for the
citizens, and a wall to defend the city. For
by חרוץ which signifies a furrow, I understand, with Mede, " that circuit bounding
out the limits of the city, whereon the
wall was builded, and antiently used to be
marked out with a plough earing a furrow
round about. By רחוב which implies a broad
place, I understand the area or plot of
ground within, whereon the houses were
to be builded." And how exactly do the
prophesy and the history correspond to each
other ! Nehemiah, we are told, during his
first administration, which lasted from the
TWENTIETH to the THIRTY SECOND year
of Artaxerxes Mnemon, not only builded
the wall, and set up the gates of Jerusalem,
but finding the city was large, and the
people were few, and the houses not builded, he made the Jews cast lots to bring one
of ten out of the other cities to dwell in
Jerusalem the holy city*; which necessarily
implies,

* Neh. vii. 4. and xi 1.

implies, that houfes were alfo to be built for their reception. Now from the fecond year of Darius Nothus, in which the commandment went forth to rebuild Jerufalem, to the thirty fecond year of Artaxerxes Mnemon, before which it was completely rebuilt, within and without, were " feven weeks" of years.

" And in the latter days of the fixty and two weeks Mefliah will be cut off." The angel does not fay fimply " fixty and two weeks," but " THE fixty and two weeks," meaning thofe he had mentioned before; and therefore the " feven" preceeding weeks muft be reckoned with them. Aquila and Symmachus render the paffage, by way of explanation , " after the feven weeks and fixty two weeks." The term " after" fignifies here, as in other places, during the continuance of that period, or fome time before the conclufion of it. Thus, " after three days I will rife again," that is, on the third day. So, " after the fixty two weeks," that is, before the expiration, towards the conclufion, or, as the original may be well rendered, " in the latter days of the fixty and two weeks." This is another demonftrative proof of the undoubted

Jewifh

Jewifh application of this prophefy to
Chrift. "The laft days, fay the Jews, are
the days of king Meffiah." And accordingly, about the time of Jefus there was
a national expectation of his coming.
Now what prophefy, except this before us,
could afford fufficient ground for fo general an expectation ? Ifaiah indeed, Joel, and
others have fpoken of " the latter days."
But who is he among the prophets, that
has directly, or even indirectly, fixed the
commencement of that decifive period ?
Daniel alone has determined the time. By
him we are affured, that within the compafs of " SEVEN weeks, SIXTY TWO weeks,
and ONE week," or four hundred and ninety
years, " from the promulgation of a commandment to rebuild Jerufalem," it fhall
be again deftroyed ; and that " in the LAT-
TER DAYS of the SIXTY TWO weeks MES-
SIAH will be CUT OFF." The LAST DAYS
therefore are the CONCLUSION of the JEW-
ISH AGE ; they are the days of the MES-
SIAH, becaufe he was to appear and be cut
off in them [52] ; andthe time intended by
the expreffion, which in other prophets is
general and indeterminate, is here particularly determined: for the Jewifh age and
the

the feventieth week are to expire together. In thefe " laft days, faid the Angel, Meffiah will be cut off." Agreeably to which we find, that " CHRIST was manifefted in the LAST TIMES, the CONCLUSION OF THE" Jewifh " AGE, to put away fin by the facrifice of himfelf*." And hiftory informs us, that within forty years after the death of Chrift both the city and the temple of Jerufalem were totally deftroyed. But of this hereafter. In the mean time we are to obferve, that Meffiah was to be condemned and put to death in a judicial manner, for fo the original word § implies. Now what but the fpirit of prophefy could forefee, that the Jews themfelves would thus endeavour to quench the light, and to cut off the hope of Ifrael? Even Pilate afked with fome amazement, though, no doubt, farcaftically, " Shall I crucify YOUR KING?" Yet " they ALL cried out, let him be crucified." And the " title of his accufation was

THE KING OF THE JEWS [53]."

It follows in the Prophefy, לו ןאי, which I render, " for they," Daniel's " people" mentioned before, " will not be his." Accordingly,

---

* 1 Peter i. 20. Heb. ix. 26. § See Lev. xvii. 14.

cordingly, " he came to his own, and his own received him not *." And Meffiah himself declared, that " he muft be reject- ed of that generation †." And again, with the addition of a moft awful threatening, " thofe mine enemies, who would not that I fhould reign over them, bring hither and flay before me ‡."

This is the very next circumftance in the angel's prophefy. " Wherefore a people of the prince that fhall come fhall deftroy the city and the fanctuary, and the end thereof fhall be with a flood ; and at the end of the war defolations are determined." The Romans are here ftyled the " people of Meffiah, the prince that fhall come[54]," becaufe they were employed in his fervice againft the Jews. Thus the Affyrian is call- ed " the rod of God's anger, and the ftaff in their hand his indignation, though he himfelf meant not fo, neither did his heart think fo, but it was in his heart to deftroy and cut off many nations ||." In like man- ner, with equal elegance and propriety, " the locuft canker-worm caterpillar and palmer-worm" are faid to be " his great ar- my §." And our Saviour himfelf, alluding

to

* John i. 2. † Luke xvii. 25. ‡ Ibid. xix. 27.
| Ifaiah x. 5—7. § Joel ii. 25.

to this very deftruction of Jerufalem by the Romans, declares that " the king, that is God, fent forth his armies *," The true meaning therefore of the paffage is plainly this. The Romans, Meffiah's armies, fhall come pouring in like fome mighty inundation, fweep away the inhabitants of Jerufalem, totally deftroy both the city and the temple, and make the whole land an utter defolation. This is the PROPHECY. And are not Jerufalem and her children, at this very day, wonderful monuments of its COMPLETION!

This train of calamities, however, was not to fall upon the devoted nation immediately. It makes the proper and diftinguifhing fubject of the " one week," called by St John " the laft time†," and the angel foretells a ftriking circumftance that was to be, as it were, the forerunner of it. " He, the prince that fhall come, fhall caufe a covenant to prevail‡ among many." The term " many" frequently fignifies all. Daniel himfelf ufes it in this fenfe. " MANY of them that fleep in the duft of the earth fhall awake," that is, all, as our Saviour

---

Matt. xxii. 7.   † John iii. 18,

‡ הגביר   See the Lexicons.

viour explains it. "ALL that are in the graves fhall come forth *." So God fays to Abraham, "A father of MANY nations have I made thee ;" which St Paul produces as a proof, to the Jews, that Abraham "is the father of us ALL †." The word has the fame meaning here. "He fhall caufe a covenant," the new covenant, of which Meffiah was to be the meffenger, "to prevail among all" nations. "This gofpel of the kingdom muft firft be publifhed among ALL nations, and then fhall the end come ‡." Here we have our Saviour's authority for the interpretation. And accordingly, in confequence of Chrift's commiffion to "go and teach all nations," the apoftles "went forth and preached every where," proclaiming the glad tidings of Meffiah's kingdom, "the kingdom of heaven," in all parts of the Roman empire. "Their found verily went into all the earth, and their words unto the ends of the world." So that even in St Paul's time "the gofpel was preached to every creature under heaven ‖."

Here

* Dan. xii. 2=John v. 28. † Gen. xvii. 4, 5.=Rom. iv. 16, 17. ‡ Matt. xxiv. 14.=Mark xiii. 10.
‖ Col. i. 12.

Here, one would think, infidelity herfelf muſt bluſh, when ſhe fees, and, if ſhe
opens her eyes, ſhe cannot but fee this feem-
ingly improbable event ſo plainly foretold,
and ſo fully accompliſhed. Let any candid Jew, any " Iſraelite indeed," confider
the author and the preachers of this new
religion, and ſay, whether the faƈt was
ſuch as lay within the reach of human
forefight and human power. If he looks
into the goſpel hiſtory, he may there find
the author of the faith betrayed by one of
his diſciples, denied by another, forſaken
by all---by thoſe very perſons he had pur-
poſely choſen to ſpread his religion in the
world---and at laſt nailed to a croſs. Were
not theſe now, both the maſter and the
fervants, bleſſed inſtruments to work with!
And yet through their means, ſo admira-
ble are the ways of providence ! this goſpel of the kingdom grew mightily and
" PREVAILED." " Behold then ! ye deſpiſers,
and wonder, and"---be perſuaded. For if
this thing were not of God, it will be im-
poſſible to ſay what is. If ye can ſtill reſiſt
the evidence of ſo ſtrong a proof, well may
ye diſbelieve, " though one roſe from the
dead."

" Then,

" Then," fays our Saviour, when the gofpel has been publifhed among all na-tions, " fhall the end" of the Jewifh age " come." For then, as the angel goes on, fpeaking of the " ONE remaining WEEK [55], in HALF of that week he fhall caufe the facrifice and oblation to ceafe; for with a wing [56], an army, of abominations he fhall caufe defolation, even till the con-fummation, and that determined fhall be poured upon the defolators."

What doubts foever might have arifen concerning the commencement of the weeks, one would have thought there could not reafonably have been any about the conclu-fion of them. The end of Jerufalem is their end alfo. This is fo exprefsly affirm-ed both by the angel and by Jefus, that no one who pays proper attention to either can difpute it. In this laft week Meffiah was to come. For " from the promulgation of a commandment to rebuild Jerufalem UNTO Meffiah the prince were to be SEVEN weeks and SIXTY TWO weeks," or SIXTY NINE in the whole. He was therefore to come in the SEVENTIETH. Our Saviour's king-dom began at his refurrection from the dead, and he took poffeffion of it at his af-cenfion cenſion into heaven. But then only was his regal power manifeſted, when he "CAME, as he himſelf expreſſes it, IN HIS KING-DOM." This coming of Meſſiah, with its neceſſary conſequence, the deſtruction of the Jewiſh temple and city, is frequently fore-told in the new teſtament. " Verily I ſay unto you, there be ſome ſtanding here who ſhall not taſte of death, till they ſee the ſon of man coming in his kingdom *. " This generation ſhall not paſs [57] till all theſe things, the coming of the ſon of man and the deſtruction of Jeruſalem, " be ful-filled +." And again, when Peter was de-ſirous to know the fate of the favorite diſciple, after he had heared his own, Jeſus replied, " If I will that he tarry till I COME, What is that to thee ‡ ? And the ſame Peter declares, " We have not followed cunningly deviſed fables, when we made known unto you the POWER and COMING of our Lord Jeſus Chriſt, but were eye-witneſſes of his MAJESTY." And then, to gain credit to his ſecond aſſertion, the ſpeedy " COMING of Jeſus Chriſt," he appeals to " a ſure word of PROPHESY [58] ---this very propheſy recorded by Daniel."

For

* Mat. xvi. 28. † Ibid. xxiv. 34. ‡ John xxi. 22.

For though other prophets had indeed predicted Messiah's coming, yet none but Daniel had fixed the time of it.

The design of his coming was to cause
the temple-service, " the sacrifice and the
oblation to cease," that is, finally, as the
word necessarily imports, when there is nothing to restrain its meaning. This he
did by causing the temple itself, the place
of sacrifice, to be destroyed. " With an
army of abominations he shall cause desolation," both in the city and the temple;
for the angel says expressly, " the people
of the prince that shall come, shall destroy
the city and the SANCTUARY." And our
Saviour foretells the same thing. " Your
HOUSE is left unto you DESOLATE; and
there shall not be left one stone upon another that shall not be thrown down +."
This destruction of the temple was, without controversy, providential. The Roman general, as might naturally be expected, labored to the utmost of his power to
save that stupendous edifice from the rage
of war, as a grace to his conquest, and as
an ornament to his empire. But in defi-
ance to all his commands, intreaties, threat-
nings,

+ Matthew xxiii. 38. and xxiii. 2.

nings, and even blows, thofe very foldiers, who before had been accuftomed to obey orders. now --- actuated by a divine en- thufiaftic impulfe *---paid no attention to their commander, but intrepidly encourag- ed each other in throwing firebrands into various parts of the temple, till at length this pride of Jewry, and of the world, was totally confumed. The deftruction of the city foon followed that of the temple, and in both the Jews perifhed without num- ber †. Well then might thefe armies be ftyled the " people of Meffiah, the prince that fhould come," when they fo punctu- ally fulfilled his word in " deftroying thofe murderers, and in burning their city."

The neceffity of this fevere difpenfation is no lefs confpicuous than the juftice of it. Nothing gave more offence to the be- liever, or afforded matter of greater triumph to the unbeliever, than the continuance of the Jewifh temple and worfhip. Hence that irreligious infult of the fcoffers, " Where is the promife of his coming ‡?" And hence thofe warm exhortations of the apoftles to their converts, " to hold faft

H   the

---

* ΔΑΙΜΟΝΠΩ ορμη—ΕΝΘΟΥΣΙΩΝΤΩΝ των ςρατιωτων.

† Jofephus, p. 1291. Edit. Hudfon. ‡ 2 Pet. iii. 4.

the profeffion of their faith without wa-
vering ; and not to forfake the affembling
of themfelves together, as the manner of
fome was, but to exhort one another" to
fteadfaftnefs in the faith, " and fo much
the more as they faw THE DAY," the day
of their Lord's advent, "APPROACHING*."
Befides, the temple and city of Jerufalem
were the vifible tokens of the THEOCRACY,
or God's fpecial government of the Jews
and of Jewdea. It was therefore neceffary
to remove thefe out of the way, that, " the
middle wall of partition being broken
down," the kingdom of heaven might be
extended, as foretold, over all nations.
This was truly, what our bleffed Saviour
himfelf emphatically calls it, " THE SIGN
--- OF THE SON OF MAN IN HEAVEN †."
And thus was " THE MOST HOLY" JESUS
folemnly " ANOINTED ; and there was
given him dominion and glory and a kingdom, that ALL people nations and languages fhould ferve him."

We muft now go back again to the prophefy. " In half of that," the feventieth
or laft " week --- with a wing of abominations he fhall caufe defolation." Wings
are

---

* Heb. x. 23—25.   † Matt. xxii. 30.

are no unufual figures for armies. "An army of abominations" then is, in the Jewifh ftyle, an army of idolaters, as "people of abominations ‡" is an idolatrous people. We are indebted to St Luke for this interpretation. For inftead of the "abomination of defolation ftanding in the holy land §," he fays, "Jerufalem encompaffed with armies *[59]." And here we cannot but obferve and pity the cool, defperate malice of that arch-infidel, Mr Collins, on this occafion. "What, fays he, can be more unaccountable, than making JESUS, who had been DEAD thirty five years, the GENERAL of the Roman army that took Jerufalem, and deftroyed the temple ✝?" The Chriftian anfwer is, that the fame JESUS, who died, ROSE again on the third day. Nor was ever any one, I prefume, fo unaccountably abfurd as to imagine, that Jefus himfelf fought perfonally againft the Jews. We find in Ifaiah this burden of Babylon. "Lift ye up a banner upon the high mountain; ---- I have commanded my fanctified ones, I have alfo called my mighty ones for my anger. ----

The

---

‡ Ezra ix. 14.   § Mat. xxiv. 15.
* Luke xxi. 20.   ✝ Scheme, &c. p. 189.

The noife of a multitude in the mountains,
like as of a great people, a tumultuous
noife of the kingdoms of nations gathered
together; THE LORD OF HOSTS MUSTER-
ETH THE HOST OF THE BATTLE.   They
COME from a far country, from the end of
heaven, even the LORD, and the weapons
of his indignation, deftroy the whole land.
--- THE DAY OF THE LORD IS AT HAND;
---BEHOLD! THE DAY OF THE LORD COM-
ETH, --- TO LAY THE LAND DESOLATE*."
This image is not only proper, but elegant
and noble.   And if God himfelf may be
thus defcribed, " muftering the hoft, and
coming to lay the land of Babylon defolate," why may not the Son of God be defcribed in the fame terms, as prefiding
over the Roman eagles, and " coming" to
the defolation of Jerufalem?   The plain
meaning therefore of the prophecy is this.
The deftruction of the holy city will be as
fignal a manifeftation of the power of
Meffiah, as if he were to come vifibly, at
the head of the Romans, " conquering and
to conquer."

The time too, in which this deftruction
was to be accomplifhed, is minutely defcribed

* Ifaiah xiii. 1—9.

fcribed by the angel. " In HALF of the" laft " WEEK he fhall caufe defolation." And it appears by Jofephus's hiftory of the Jewifh war, compared with Ptolemy's canon, that from Vefpafian's marching into Jewdea to the deftruction of Jerufalem were about THREE YEARS AND A HALF [60].

Full SEVENTEEN HUNDRED YEARS has Jerufalem now continued in her defolations --- and muft continue, as the angel proceeds, " even till the confummation, and that determined fhall be poured upon the defolators." That is, in the language of our Saviour, " Jerufalem fhall be trodden down of the Gentiles until the times of the Gentiles be fulfilled *." And then, as St Paul obferves, when " the fulnefs of the Gentiles is come in, all Ifrael," both Jews and Gentiles, " fhall be faved †."

CONCLUSION.

I have now gone through the feveral particulars of thefe illuftrious and moft important predictions. We do not here read of one fingle point only, but of a long train of events to be accomplifhed within

H 3   certain

* Luke xxi. 24.   † Rom. xi. 25, 26.

certain fucceffive periods. And we affirm,
that each of thefe events has been accomplifhed in its feafon. We affirm likewife,
that all the particulars of thefe predictions,
fo far as Chriftianity is concerned, were
fulfilled by JESUS, who is therefore, as
we believe, THE MESSIAH.

It is not difficult, nor indeed uncom-
mon, to find out likeneffes where there are
none, or at leaft where none were intended. But will you fay, that the correfpon-
dence, in fo many points, between MES-
SIAH and JESUS, is fanciful, or the effect
of mere chance? This, I prefume, cannot be juftly faid. Here then are PROPHE-
SIES, and here is the COMPLETION of every
part of them, to which if we can make no
reafonable objection, we ought to admit
" the everlafting gofpel of the bleffed God,"
and to endeavour to know and to do his
facred will, accounting this to be the beft,
the only foundation of our prefent hopes,
and of our future happinefs. " FOR
OTHER FOUNDATION CAN NO MAN LAY
THAN THAT IS LAID, WHICH IS
JESUS THE CHRIST*."

* 1 Cor. iii. 11.

NOTES.

N O T E S.

[1] THOSE writers, who pretend to prove the truth of the Chriftian religion independently of the Old Teftament, deferve our pity. CHRISTI-ANITY, as the very term declares, is relative, and fuppofes a CHRIST foretold. To talk therefore of a Chriftianity independent of " the law and the prophets," on which alone it can have a reafonable foundation, is precifely the fame abfurdity as to talk of a NEW teftament without the OLD one.

[2] The GOLDEN IMAGE, erected by this mighty prince, feems to have been dedicated to himfelf. Sulpitius Severus directly afferts it. "Nabuchodonofor, elatus rebus fecundis, ftatuam SIBI auream immenfæ magnitudinis pofuit, adoraríque eam ut facram effigiem precepit." p. 68. ed. Elz, 1656. And it is fairly implied in the hiftory of the tranfaction. " Nebuchadnezzar the king made an image of gold — and fent to gather together all the great men of his empire to come to the dedication of it." Dan. iii. 1, 2. If the king had not dedicated this image to himfelf, the facred writer would, moft probably, have mentioned the name of the deitv. If it were dedicated to himfelf, there was no occafion to fpecify it, as it may be eafily collected from the following paffages. " There are certain Jews — thefe

men, O king, have not regarded thee, they ferve not thy gods, NOR worſhip the golden image which thou haſt ſet up. — Nebuchadnezzar ſaid unto them, Is it true? Do ye not ſerve my gods, NOR worſhip the golden image which I have ſet up?" Dan. iii. 12—14. In both theſe places Nebuchadnezzar's IMAGE is expreſsly diſtinguiſhed from his GODS. And therefore if it were not a repreſentative of one of his gods, it muſt have been the repreſentative of himſelf. — Should any one think it improbable, that after his prophetic dream, he could be ſo infatuated as to deify himſelf, I will ſhew the probability of it from a ſimilar faſt. This very prince " was at reſt in his houſe, and floriſhing in his palace," when, in conſequence of his pride and preſumption, " he ſaw a dream which made him afraid, and his thoughts and the viſions of his head troubled him." The meaning of the dream was, according to Daniel's interpretation of it, " That the king ſhould be driven from men, and have his dwelling among the beaſts of the field, and that ſeven years ſhould paſs over him, till he knew, or acknowledged, that the Moſt High ruleth in the kingdom of men, and giveth it to whomſoever he will," Dan. iv. 3—25. Who would think it probable, that, after ſuch an expreſs admonition, Nebuchadnezzar would be guilty of ſo great a crime, as could deſerve ſo ſevere a puniſhment! And yet, " at the end of twelve months he was walking in the palace of the kingdom of Babylon, and proudly ſaid, Is not this great Babylon, that I have built for the houſe of the kingdom, by the might of my power, and for the honour of my majeſty?" He had ſcarce finiſhed, when the former prediction was repeated and fulfilled. Verſe 29—33.

[3] " Veritus

[3] " Veritus ne more hominum non vera, fed pla-
cita regi ex fomnio conjectarent, VISA SUPPRIMIT,
popofcitque ab eis, ut, fi vera in his divinatio effet,
fomnium ipfum fibi dicerent; tum demum interpreta-
tioni eorum crediturum, fi prius enuntiando fomnium
artis periculum feciffent." Sulpit. Sever. p. 65. Ci-
cero underftood the true fecret of pagan divination.
" Tota res eft inventa FALLACIIS, aut ad QUÆSTUM,
aut ad SUPERSTITIONEM, aut ad ERROREM." De
divin. lib. ii. 41. The Jewifh prophets give the
fame account of it. Ifaiah in particular, fpeaking of
the Chaldean diviners, introduces Jehovah declaring,
that he " FRUSTRATETH THE TOKENS OF THE
LIARS." Chap. xliv. 25.

[4] Nebuchadnezzar had this dream in " the SE-
COND year of his reign." Confequently he was not
the Nebuchadnezzar mentioned in the firft chapter.
For there we read, that Daniel and his companions
were to be nourifhed " THREE YEARS, that AT THE
END thereof they might ftand before the king," ver. 5.
And we are told afterwards, that " AT THE END OF
THE DAYS that the king had faid that he fhould bring
them in, then the prince of the eunuchs brought them
in before Nebuchadnezzar," ver. 18. The firft Nebuchadnezzar therefore was NABOPOLLASSAR, and the
fecond was NABOCOLLASSAR in Ptolemy's canon.
" Ebræis tam PATER quam FILIUS vocatur NABU-
CHODONOSORUS. In libro luchafin diftinguuntur.
' Ætas quinta. Deportatio Ifraelis in Babel per Ne-
buchadnezarum FILIUM Nebuchadnezari.' ' Pater
PRIMUS denominatur, filius MAGNUS.' In canone
fatis diverfa funt eorum nomina." Marfhami can.
chron. p. 574. edit. Lipf. 1676.

[5] It

[5] It is remarkable that Tully enumerates the diviners almoſt in the ſame order as we find them in Daniel, " haruſpices, et fulguratores, et interpretes oſten-
torum, et augures, et ſortilegos, et CHALDÆOS."
And yet he had before ſaid expreſsly, " CHALDÆI
non ex ARTIS ſed ex GENTIS vocabulo nominati."
De divin. i. 1, et ii. 53. The paſſage therefore in
Daniel may be thus interpreted. The king ſent for
" the magicians, and the aſtrologers, and the ſorcerers,
who were Chaldeans." Accordingly, the converſation
is carried on between the king and the Chaldeans.
And Daniel, when he ſpeaks in his own perſon, omits
them, reckoning only " the wiſemen, the aſtrologers,
the magicians, and the ſoothſayers." Theſe jugglers
therefore, by whatever titles dignified or diſtinguiſhed,
and the Chaldeans, are the ſame perſons.

[6] Another reaſon may be aſſigned why this acci-
dental circumſtance ſhould deſerve no notice, becauſe
if the Greeks had chanced to have been repreſented by
ſilver, an application is ready. " Cui gloriæ ut etiam exercitus ornamenta convenirent, phaleras equorum, et arma
militum, ARGENTO inducit [Alexander]; exercitum-
que ſuum, ab ARGENTEIS CLYPEIS, ARGYRASPIDAS
appellavit." Juſtin. p. 111. ed. Amſtel. 1644.

[7] Not exactly TEN, but, in a ſymbolic ſenſe, all
the pagan provinces of the empire. Indeed " the το
τριτον typi," as Mr Mede expreſſes it, the decorum of
the repreſentation naturally leads us to this ſenſe ; for
as by the term TOES, in their literal ſenſe, the prophet
unqueſtionably means the full complement of toes on
the feet of the image, ſo in their repreſentative capacity
they muſt denote the full complement of the pagan

ſtates or kingdoms of Rome. The learned and ingenious Dr Hurd, though he generally follows his pre-
deceſſors in this argument, yet he leaves them here,
and, inſtead of hunting for TEN kingdoms or ſtates, he
plainly calls them " MANY diſtinct kingdoms." Biſhop
Warburton's Lecture, p. 399.

[8] So Pſalm xxxix. 7. " He HEAPETH up [heaps]
and knoweth not who ſhall gather THEM." Thucy-
dides has the very ſame mode of expreſſion. Η μιλλον-
τις ΠΟΛΕΜΗΣΕΙΝ, η ιν ΑΥΤΩ ηδη οντις. I. 13. In both
theſe paſſages the NOUN is evidently IMPLIED in the
VERB.

[9] Our public tranſlation ſays, " of the STRENGTH
of the iron." But this very circumſtance is expreſſed
in the next clauſe, and by a different term. The Greek
verſion has απο της ΡΙΖΗΣ, which ſuits the place exactly, the provinces deriving their political exiſtence from
the parent country. The vulgar Latin, Syriac, and
Arabic tranſlations give the ſame ſenſe.

[10] Luke ii. 1—6. Εγινιτο δι ιν ταις ημιραις ικαναις,
ιξηλθι δογμα παρα Καισαγος ΑΥΓΟΥΣΤΟΥ, απογραφισθαι
πασαν την οικουμινην. (Αυτη η απογραφη πρωτη ιγινιτο ιγι-
μονιυοντος της Συριας Κυρηνιου.) Και ιπορινοντο παντις απογραφισθαι, ικαςος ιις την ιδιαν πολιν. Ανιβη δι και Ιωσηφ κ.τ.λ.
The Engliſh tranſlation of this paſſage ſeems totally in-
defenſible. Whatever the conſtruction of the paren-
theſis may be, the meaning is plain and obvious, it being the deſign of the evangeliſt to diſtinguiſh this inrollment from another mentioned Acts v. 37. and which
was made by " Cyrenius governor of Syria." I ſup-
poſe an ellipſis, and that the relative της is implied in
αυτη. The whole paſſage therefore may be thus tranſ-
lated.

lated. " It came to pafs in thofe days [the days of
Herod the king of Jewdea, 1. 5.] that there went out
a decree from Cæfar AUGUSTUS that the whole land,"
every part of Herod's dominion, " fhould be inrolled.
(THIS inrollment was before" THAT " of Cyrenius
governor of Syria.) And all went to be inrolled, every
one into his own city. And Jofeph alfo went up from
Galilee, out of the city of Nazareth, into Jewdea, unto
the city of David, which is called Bethlehem, becaufe
he was of the houfe and lineage of David, to be inrolled with Mary his efpoufed wife, being great with
child." St Luke himfelf ufes the word οικουμενη in the
fame fenfe elfewhere. " Men's hearts failing them for
fear and for looking after thofe things which are coming on τη οικουμενη" [not the earth, but] " the land" of
Jewdea. Chap. xxi. 26. See ver. 21, 23. And, perhaps, the word has the fame meaning Acts xi. 28. As
to the word πρωτη, that may as well be ufed for προ as
εχατη for υπερον. St Mark, fpeaking of the woman
which had had feven hufbands, fays, εχατη παντων, " AF-
TER all the woman died," unqueftionably not THE LAST
of all. Compare Mark xii. 22. with Matt. xxii. 27. and
Luke xx. 32. So 2 Maccab. vii. 42. εχατη των υιων,
" AFTER the fons the mother died," not the laft of the
fons. As to the ellipfis (if the word της has not indeed
flipped out of the text by accident) it is not very harfh.
" THIS inrollment" neceffarily implies fome OTHER
—— which was THAT " of Cyrenius governor of Syria." There is a paffage in Jofephus, which, in the
opinion of fome learned writers, relates to this inrollment mentioned by St Luke. The whole ftory is fo
long, that I muft refer the reader to it, Antiq. xvii. c.
2. § 6. and to Dr Lardner's obfervations upon it, Cre-
dib. p. 367—369, and will only add two remarks to

thofe of the learned doctor. 1. When Jofephus fays, that " all the Jews, except fix thoufand, fwore to be faithful to Cæsar and the interefts of the king," I fufpect he does not really mean, though he would be underftood to mean, king Herod, but Cæfar himfelf. The Jewifh writers frequently ufe the noun for the pronoun. Thus John iv. 1. " When the Lord knew how the Pharifees had heard that Jesus made and baptifed more difciples than John." Here the Lord and Jefus are the fame perfon. So in Jofephus Cæfar and the king may be one and the fame. When I confider the very bad terms on which Herod now ftood with Cæfar, as we learn from Jofephus himfelf, I cannot be eafily brought to believe, that Cæfar would include Herod in the oath of fidelity. If that had been indeed the cafe, it would have been more natural to fay ευνοησαι Καισαρι κ̀ βασιλﬖ, than κ̀ τοις βασιλεως πραγμασι. There was at this time a general expectation of a new king. The Jews claimed this king to themfelves. This eafily accounts for the imperial decree, that all the Jewifh nation (παντος του Ιουδαικου) fhould fwear to be well affected to Cæfar and his affairs. It is not to be expected, that fuch a bigotted Jew as Jofephus would be explicit on this occafion. His ill-will to the gofpel (though Mr Whifton has been pleafed to chriften him) fhall immediately appear, and I think it is a clear proof that the latter part of the oath to Cæfar has a reference to St Luke's inrollment. For, 2. fome of the Pharifees, who had refufed to take the oath, had likewife predicted, according to Jofephus, that the Jewifh kingdom would be transferred from Herod and his family to a new king, who, having all things in his own power, would grant to Bagoas, a court eunuch, the capacity of marriage and of having children." I appeal to the

reader,

reader, whether the eunuch and his children are not here brought upon the ftage merely as a banter upon Chriftians, whofe Meffiah was born of a VIRGIN. If this be fo, the paffage in Jofephus is parallel with the hiftory of the birth of Jefus as related by St Matthew and St Luke.

[11] Though the name of Grotius fhould be ever mentioned with refpect, yet his notions, when unfavorable to the caufe of truth, may very properly be cenfured; efpecially as the adverfary has availed himfelf of his authority in attacking Chriftianity. The STONE, according to Grotius, " is the Roman PEOPLE who originated from a MOUNTAIN, namely, the Palatine." But the ftone and the mountain muft be. homogeneal. Take then the terms either figuratively or literally. If the ftone is a fymbol and reprefents a people, the mountain muft do fo too. If the mountain be underftood literally, fo muft the ftone. Both muft be fymbols, or neither. To tell us therefore, that MOUNT Palatine produced the ROMANS, is in fober truth as ftrange, and as wide from the purpofe, as if he had told us, that this fame mountain produced a moufe.

The truth is, this great and good man was under the power of a fatal prejudice. Proteftant writers had connected the ftone's conqueft with the deftruction of Papal Rome, not reflecting, that the mountain reprefents the Jewifh church, and confequently that the ftone, " cut out of the mountain," can only fignify Chrift and his apoftles, or at moft the Jewifh converts to Chriftianity. Grotius therefore, having projected an alliance between Papifts and Proteftants, not only rejected the proteftant conceit, but the fober opinion of

Pagans,

Pagans, Jews, and Christians, who agree in the descrip-
tion of the four empires. His scheme is this. The
golden head, silver breast, and brasen belly, signify the
kingdoms of Babylon, Persia, and ALEXANDER; the
legs and feet the KINGDOM of the SELEUCIDÆ and
LAGIDÆ; and the stone, as we have seen, that of the
Romans. Now the distinguishing of Alexander's empire from that of his successors, is the most unlearned
notion that ever entered into the head of a man of
learning. " PORPHYRY, as Mr Mede assures us, was
the first broacher of it." Page 743. Bishop Chandler
says, " No ANCIENT HISTORIAN ever confined the
Greek empire to Alexander's person, or made a distinct
empire of the four kingdoms that arose upon his death."
Def. p. 99. And another respectable prelate asserts,
that " ALL ANCIENT AUTHORS speak of the kingdom
of Alexander and his successors as one and the same
kingdom." Bishop Newton, Vol. I. p. 416. Tacitus,
who, I think, has not been produced on this occasion,
has a most remarkable passage. " Dum ASSYRIOS penes
MEDOS que et PERSAS oriens fuit, despectissima pars ser-
vientium [Judæi]. Postquam MACEDONES præpotuere
———— etc. ROMANORUM primus Cn. Pompeius Judæos domuit." Histor. l. v. s. 8, 9. Here the history
is a perfect tally to the prophecy, as it represents the
four great empires in their successive relation to the
Jews. We need not therefore be surprised at the difference between Daniel and Grotius, when we reflect,
that the prophet has interpreted Nebuchadnezzar's
dream, and the critic his own.

[12] This is the true meaning of that famous text,
" Thou art Peter, &c." which the Romish builders
have made the foundation of Papal authority. Our

Saviour

Saviour is inquiring of his difciples what the rumors of
the people were concerning him. ' Whom do men
fay that I am ? a fon of man ?" a man like themfelves ?
" Is not this the fon of Jofeph ?" Luke iv. 22. John vi. 42.
They reply, " Some fay John the baptift, fome Elias,
and others Jeremias, or one of the prophets. He faith
unto them, But whom fay ye that I am? Simon Peter anfwered," by divine revelation, " Thou art
Christ, the Son of the living God. Then
Jefus faid unto him, Bleffed art thou, Simon Bar-jonah,
for flefh and blood hath not revealed it unto thee, but
my Father who is in heaven. And I fay unto thee,
for thou art Peter *, that on that rock * I will build
my church, and the gates of death fhall not prevail
againft it," Matt. xvi. 13—18. Nothing was more
ufual with our bleffed Lord than to raife matter of doc-
trine and moral inftruction from the things at hand §.
It was, if I may fo fay, his peculiar ftyle. Thus in
this very chapter, the difciples having forgotten to take
bread, he fays to them, " Beware of the leaven of
the Pharifees and of the Sadducees," ver. 5, 6. that is,
the hypocritical doctrines of the one, and the licentious
doctrines of the other. So to Peter himfelf, in the
character of a fisher, " Thou fhalt catch men,"
Luke v. 10. What would the Romanift have more?
In the firft text there is a plain allufion to Peter's name,
in the laft to his profession. Our Saviour does not
mean by the " rock " either Peter himfelf, or his confeffion, but the great truth contained in that confeffion, That " Jefus is the Chrift the Son of the living God," communicated to Peter by divine revelation;
" Flefh

---

* πιτρο·, a ftone, πιτρα, a rock.

§ See Dr Jortin on the Chriftian religion, p. 213—216.
and from thence to p. 221 in the notes.

" Flesh and blood hath not revealed it unto thee, but my Father who is in heaven." This is a clear proof, that he did not ask, Whom do men say, that I, THE SON OF MAN, am? for that would have been a previous declaration of his Messiahship; but he puts two distinct questions, " Whom do men say that I am? a son of man ‡?" To which questions Peter's answer has a plain reference. " Thou art Christ, the Son of the living God." Jesus accepts the character, and makes it the foundation of his church.

[13] Bishop Chandler (the author of an excellent Defence of Christianity against Collins) has given a very strange interpretation of this passage, and, what is worse, he has made our Saviour himself the author of it. " THE KINGDOM OF GOD, says Christ, or ALL THE ADVANTAGES of the Messiah's coming, SHALL BE TAKEN FROM YOU, AND GIVEN TO A NATION BRINGING FORTH THE FRUITS THEREOF. FOR WHOSOEVER SHALL FALL AGAINST THIS STONE (as one of your prophets * predicted) SHALL BE BROKEN; BUT, I add, from another prophet †, something more grievous for those that shall break you, ON WHOMSOEVER IT SHALL FALL, it will GRIND HIM TO POWDER. The kingdom of the STONE shall bruise the Jews that stumbled at Christ's first coming; but the kingdom of the MOUNTAIN, when manifested, shall beat the feet of the monarchical statue to dust, and leave no remains of the fourth monarchy in its last, and degenerate, state." Page 105.

This is directly opposite to our Saviour's meaning. The same STONE that was to break the Jews, who

I   fell

‡ See Luke iv. 22. and John vi. 42. and elsewhere.
* Isaiah viii.   † Dan. ii. 34, 35.

fell againſt it, was to grind the Gentiles to powder. Nothing is ſaid about the MOUNTAIN. Chriſt aſſerts two things. 1. " That the kingdom of God," or all the advantages of the Meſſiah's coming, " ſhall be taken away from the Jews." 2. " That the kingdom of God," or all the advantages of the Meſſiah's coming, " ſhall be given to the Romans." In ſupport of theſe aſſertions, he produces the evidence of two Jewiſh pro- phets. " FOR (ſays he, as Iſaiah predicted) whoſoever ſhall fall againſt this STONE ſhall be broken; BUT on whomſoever IT ſhall fall (as Daniel foretold) IT ſhall grind him to powder." I will leave the paſſage to ſpeak for itſelf, only obſerving, that, if the coming of Chriſt was to deſtroy the fourth monarchy, it could not receive ANY ADVANTAGES from his coming. There is a very material difference between deſtroying the PAGANISM and deſtroying the MONARCHY of Rome.

[14] Acts xi. 26. So I tranſlate the word χρηματισαι, 1. becauſe this is its uſual ſignification throughout the new teſtament. 2. If the diſciples had been left to themſelves, they would, moſt probably, have taken their name from JESUS, and have been called Jeſuits. 3. Becauſe this fact was foretold by Iſaiah. " The GENTILES ſhall ſee thy righteouſneſs, and all kings thy glory; and THOU SHALT BE CALLED BY A NEW NAME, WHICH THE MOUTH OF THE LORD SHALL NAME." chap. lxii. 2.

[15] Euſebius tells us, that as Conſtantine was marching againſt Maxentius, having prayed to God for his aſſiſtance, he ſaw in the afternoon the trophy of a croſs placed in heaven itſelf above the ſun ‡, with this

‡ ʜ ɑυτʜ ουρɑɴ υπιρκɑμɴοɴ του ʜλɪοɴ ſɑυρου τροπɑɪοɴ.

this infcription annexed to it, ΤΟΥΤΩ [τροπαιω] ΝΙΚΑ."
Life of Conftantine. i. 28.   This was a fymbolic
vifion, denoting, 1. Conftantine's victory over Maxentius, and, 2. the triumph of Chriftianity over Paganifm, the principal object intended.   The fun, the
great ruler in the natural world, is the known fymbol
of the fupreme ruler in the political.   The crofs, the
inftrument of crucifixion, ftands here for the perfon
crucified.   And the crofs placed above the fun, fignifies, that " Chrift crucified is King of kings, and Lord
of lords."   This was Conftantine's idea of the vifion ;
for in memorial of his victory over Maxentius, and of
the conqueft of Chriftianity over Paganifm, he erected
before his palace an image of himfelf with a crofs placed
above his head (το μεν σωτηριον υπερκειμενον της αυτου
κιφαλης) and a wounded dragon under his feet."] Life
of Conftantine iii. 3.]   Eufebius explains the device
in the fame manner, and attributes it to a divine fug-
geftion.   The propriety of the vifion is evident. " Re-
ligio tota CASTRENSIS (fays Tertullian, Apol. c. 16.)
SIGNA veneratur, SIGNA jurat, & diis omnibus PRÆ-
PONIT."   Another ENSIGN therefore was exhibited
to Conftantine, SUPERIOR to all the tutelary deities of
the pagan armies.   For (to borrow the expreffive language of St Paul) " CHRIST having fpoiled principali-
ties and powers, he made a fhew of them openly,
TRIUMPHING OVER THEM BY HIS CROSS." [Col.
ii. 15.]   Some modern writers, prejudiced, perhaps, by
the popifh ufe of the SIGN of the crofs, which has no
relation to Conftantine's SIGN, have done their beft to
explain away the miraculous part of the vifion, for
which, I think, Chriftianity owes them no thanks.
But our religionifts are now growing very refined in

their

their notions. For my own part, I not only admit
the fact but the miracle too, being perfuaded that it
greatly contributed to the completion of a remarkable
prophefy recorded by Ifaiah.   " A little one fhall become a thoufand, and a fmall one a ftrong nation. I
the Lord will haften it in its time." Ifaiah lx.22. The
Converfion of the Roman empire was, doubtlefs, " the
Lord's doing, and " therefore it ought to be " marvellous in our eyes."

[16] So Jer. xii. 9. and Ezek. xxxiv. " the beafts
of the field" are ftyled in the Targum " the kings of
the heathen and their armies."   The Greek tranflators
call them θηρια, wild-beafts.   So in Daniel the Greek
has the fame word θηρια.   Yet in other places, where
the term היה ftands for other perfons, the LXX ufe
the term ζωα, which fignifies animals or living crea-
tures.   Thus Ezek. i. 5, 13, &c. and Ezek. x. 20. So
likewife Pfal. lxviii. 10. where our tranflation is, "thy
CONGREGATION hath dwelt therein."   St John, in the
Revelation, obferves the fame diftinction.   The perfecuting power is ftyled θηριον conftantly.   But the repre-
fentatives of fome other beings are called ζωα, which
our tranflators have ftrangely rendered BEASTS, though
a MAN is one of them.

[17] Our public tranflation fays, " and it was lifted
up from the earth."   But how then did " it ftand upon
feet as a man?"   The tranflation in the margin is the
true one.   For, as Grotius has obferved, " fæpe Chal-
dæis, ut et Hebræis, copula vim habet relativi."

[18] In many places, where only TWO are meant,
the Hebrew word is in the plural number, or, as fome
gram-

grammarians call it, the dual, without the numeral for
two. Thus Gen. xxvii. 36. "he hath fupplanted me
thefe [פעמים times] two times." So Lev. xii. 5. " fhe
fhall be unclean [שבעים weeks] two weeks." So likewife Dan. vii. 25. עדנין times are, confeffedly, " two
times." And the plural number is fo ufed in the place
before us. Elfe, how could the lion ftand like a man?

[19] " Les Perfes ont exercé la domination la plus
fevére, et la plus cruelle que l'on connoiffe. Les fup-
plices ufitez parmi eux font horreur à ceux qui les
lifent." Calmet on Dan. How ftrangely does the fpirit
of Popery affect the heads, and harden the hearts, of
the beft and greateft men! Here this learned Bene-
dictine, like a dutiful fon of Holy Church, roundly
afferts, that the Perfians have exercifed the moft fevere,
and the moft cruel dominion that we know of. And
yet he himfelf knew of the domination of Papal Rome,
the moft fevere and cruel we can conceive, being a
dominion over the confciences as well as bodies of
men. He fays too, that the punifhments ufed among
the Perfians beget horror in thofe who read of them.
They muft indeed beget horror even in the breaft of
an inquifitor. But what then can be faid for the punifhments of the holy office of Inquifition, which are fo
exquifitely fevere, fo artificially cruel, that the only
merciful part of them is putting the fufferers to death?

[20] The number THREE does not always fignify
that determinate number, but fometimes an indeterminate, and nothing can be more unreafonable than to
interpret fymbolical numbers literally. " Elifha, we
are told, 2 Kings xiii. 18, 19. faid to the king of Ifrael,
Take arrows, and fmite upon the ground. And he

fmote

fmote THRICE, and ftayed. Then the man of God
was wroth with him, and faid, Thou fhouldeft have
fmitten five or fix times, then hadft thou fmitten Syria
till thou hadft confumed it; whereas now thou fhalt
fmite Syria" but " THRICE." That is, Thou fhalt
only obtain a partial victory over the Syrians, and not
a compleat one. And in the place before us the oppofition, as I have obferved, between three and much,
plainly fhews, that by three we are to underftand a
few. In other places the word has a contrary figniti-
cation, and denotes many, great, excellent. Thus
St Paul " befought the Lord THRICE," that is, many
times, that fomething difagreeable might depart from
him. 2 Cor. xii. 8. In Proverbs, chap. xxii. v. 20. the
wifeman fays to his fon, " Have I not written unto
thee שלישים THREE things," that is, as our tranflators
fay, excellent things. Compare Prov. viii. 6. and Hof.
viii. 12. So שליש a THIRD fignifies frequently a great
man. See 1 Kings ix. 22. 2 Kings vii. 2, &c. And
the Pope's TRIPLE CROWN feems to be neither more
nor lefs than the SYMBOL of ΤΡΙΣΜΕΓΙΣΤΟΣ.

[21] Grotius fays, " Quatuor capita fuccreverant
loco unius." But the beaft with one head is evidently
a creature of his own making, for Daniel confines his
reprefentation to the ftate of the Greek empire under
its four heads. Indeed in another vifion he defcribes
the fame empire in its two ftates, the beaft appearing
at firft with one horn, and afterwards with four. And
it is exprefsly faid, " The great horn is the firft emperor," (I fay the firft EMPEROR, for Alexander was
not the firft king of Macedon). " Now that being
broken, whereas four ftood for it," that is, inftead of
it, " four kingdoms will ftand up out of the nation."

Our

Our learned countryman Mr Mede, expofing the opinion of Porphyry and his followers, who make two
diftinct empires out of the one empire of Alexander and
his fuccefsors, thus exprefses his own fentiments.
" Contra hanc interpretationem fic infurgo. Quod
unicâ beftiâ adumbratum eft, id unicum eft regnum,
et non duo regna; fcilicet alioquin unica beftia efset
duæ beftiæ; quod ab omni ratione alienum eft. Jam
vero omne regnum Græcorum, tam Alexandri quam
fuccefsorum ejus, unicâ beftiâ adumbratur. Ergo, etc.
Minorem leges apud Danielem, cap. viii. vers. 20, 21, 22.
' Aries (inquit angelus) bicornis, quem vidifti, funt
reges Mediæ et Perfiæ; Hircus autem ille villofus eft
rex Græciæ; Cornu autem magnum interjectum oculis
ejus eft rex primus.' (Audin' hic regem PRIMUM? ut
rex PRIMUS et reges SECUNDI non de diverfis dici
pofsunt regnis, fed uno eodemque.) Pergit; " atque
hoc effracto, quòd confurgent quatuor pro illo, quatuor regna ex gente funt afsurrectura, fed non cum
robore illius.' Hîc clarifsimum eft Alexandrum cum
fuccefsoribus fuis fuifse unius ejufdemque hirci cornua;
ideoque unius regni poteftates. Ecquis jam dixerit
BESTIAM et CORNUA EJUS efse DUAS BESTIAS? Me
judice, IPSE merebitur ILLIS annumerari, ne TERTIA
defit BESTIA." Page 715.

[22] All the tranflations agree in faying, that the
fourth beaft was " DIVERSE from all that were before
it." But as the prophet fet out with telling us, that
" the four beafts were DIVERSE one from another,'
we can hardly fuppofe, that he would here introduce
a very ufelefs tautology, and inform us again, that the
fourth beaft was different from his predecefsors. " Satis
miror (fays St Jerome) quòd cum fuprà Leænam, &

I 4   urfum,

urfum, & pardum, in tribus regnis pofuerit, Romanum regnum nulli beftiæ compararit, nifi forte ut formidolo-fam faceret beftiam, vocabulum tacuit, ut quicquid fero-cius cogitaverimus in beftiis, hocRomanos intelligamus." But the fourth beaft was not only different from the other three, but was likewife COPIED from them, (for this fenfe of the original word fee Deut. xvii. 18. and Joſh. viii. 32.) that is, as St John informs us, " a LEOPARD with the feet of a BEAR and the mouth of a LION, and fo, with its "ten horns" it was a proper reprefentative of the Roman empire, which included, in the idea of the Romans themfelves, THE WHOLE WORLD. .

[23] The number " three," as I have already ob-ferved, does not always import a determinate number, but fometimes few, fometimes many, as the context requires. In the place before us it feems to be ufed in the latter fenfe. I fhall only obferve farther, that " three of the ten horns being plucked up," SEVEN remain, which, as a fymbolic number, denote the full complement of the pagan provinces of the empire, for the little horn does not belong to them.

[24] " Not THROWN DOWN, as we of late have it. Vulgar Lat. donec throni pofiti funt; LXX et Theo-dotion, ιως οτου θϱϑνοι ετιθησαν. עד די כרסין רמיו Chald. et fic רמה ufurpatum de folio invenias apud Chald. Paraph. Jer. i. v. 15. וירמון ubi in Hebræo eft ובתבו Septuag. και θησουσιν." Mede, p. 762.

[25] Nothing is more ufual with the facred writers, than to fpeak of a perfon in the abftract. Thus St Paul fays, that " Chrift Jefus is made unto us righte-
                                                    oufnefs,

ousness, and sanctification, and redemption;" that is, a justifier, sanctifier, and redeemer, 1 Cor. i. 30. The term " judgement" is here used in the same sense. The antient of days is the only judge, for " the son of man was brought near before HIM." It is said indeed, ver. 26. " the judgement shall sit, and THEY shall take away his dominion;" but the meaning is, the judgement shall sit, and his dominion shall be taken away. Two political solemnities are alluded to in the vision. 1. That of an eastern monarch sitting in judgement to decide some cause of great importance to his subjects. And, 2. that of his associating the prince royal into the sovereignty with himself. The cause to be determined was of the greatest consequence. The question was no less than, Who are the church of God ? the Jews or the Christians ? But how was this cause to be decided ? The Jews had been, confessedly, the true church of God, and they were now possessed of the temple and city of Jerusalem, the standing, visible tokens of the theocracy. As to the Christians, they had nothing to shew, on their behalf, but their miracles, their sufferings, and their patience; poor arguments to " a perverse and crooked generation ! " Their appeal then could only be to heaven, " to God the judge of all." There they were sure of a favorable hearing. Accordingly the antient of days did sit as judge—the prophetic books were opened——judgement was given to the Christians, the saints of the most high—the Jews were destroyed as blasphemers and enemies of God and his Christ—Messiah, the Son of God, was seated on the throne prepared for him in heaven—and the saints possessed the kingdom. Here was a fair end to the controversy. " When ye have lifted up the son of man, then shall ye know," that is, it shall be known, " that

I am "

I am" he. John viii. 28. For if the deſtruction of
Jeruſalem were the predicted conſequence of cutting
off Meſſiah, it was likewiſe the irrefragable " SIGN
OF THE SON OF MAN IN HEAVEN."

[26] Some of the Jews underſtand the paſſage in
the ſame ſenſe. " One of the thrones, they ſay, is for
Meſſiah [the ſon of] David."

[27] " The word which we tranſlate here plurally
is, as it is pointed in the original, of the ſingular
number, namely, חֵיוָתָא ; whereas if it were the plural, it ſhould be חֵיוָתָא ; for that, ſay the Chaldee
grammarians, is the difference between the ſingular
and the plural emphatic, that the one has ſcheva [:]
in the penultima, the other has camets [ָ]. And ſo
we render חֵיוָתָא with ſcheva ſingularly [beaſt] twice
in the following verſes of this chapter, viz. 19 & 23."
Mede, page 780. I lay no ſtreſs on the points. I follow a ſurer guide, the context. But it was not improper to produce this authority, to ſhew that I am
not ſingular in my tranſlation of the word. Whether
I am right in the application, or not, muſt be left to
the reader.

[28] Theſe REMAINS ſeem to be the ELECT ſpoken
of by our bleſſed Saviour, Matt. xxiv. 22. " Except
thoſe days [of the great tribulation of the Jews] ſhould
be ſhortened, there ſhould no fleſh be ſaved ; but for
the elect's ſake thoſe days ſhall be ſhortened ;" or, as
St Mark expreſſes it, " except that the Lord had
ſhortened thoſe days, no fleſh ſhould be ſaved ; but for
the elect's ſake, whom he hath choſen, he hath ſhortened

ened the days." chap. xiii. 20. He means the years of
Daniel's feventieth week deftined for the deftruction
of the city and people of Jerufalem, which were fhort-
ened and reduced to three and a half. " In one week,
even in HALF of the week, he fhall caufe defolation."
Thefe remains were elected and faved from the general
carnage of that deftructive war, to continue down, to
lateft ages, a ftanding teftimony to the truth of prophecy.

[29] Much has been written ABOUT this famous
prophecy. To underftand the true defign and meaning of it, we muft obferve, that, befides a TRIBAL
and TEMPORAL fcepter, which Jewdah had in common with his brethren, he had alfo another of a
LARGER extent, and of A MORE IMPORTANT nature.
" DAN fhall judge his people AS ONE of the tribes,
or fcepters, of Ifrael." ver. 16. But unto JEWDAH it
is moreover faid, " THY FATHER'S CHILDREN SHALL
BOW DOWN BEFORE THEE." And then it follows,
" THE SCEPTER SHALL NOT DEPART FROM JEW-
DAH." Here are plainly TWO diftinct fcepters. And
therefore to fhew which of the two was intended in
the prophecy concerning JEWDAH, it is immediately
added, " for OF HIM " (that is the meaning of the
phrafe " from between his feet") fhall come " THE
LAWGIVER." We meet with the fame thing elfewhere. " Jewdah prevailed above his brethren, for
of him fhall come" (fo it fhould be tranflated) " the
chief ruler." 1 Ch. v. 2. And David fays, " God hath
chofen Jewdah to be the ruler." 1 Ch. xxviii. 4. Who
this is we learn from the moft unexceptionable authority, that of the whole body of the chief priefts and
fcribes." For when Herod demanded of them, "Where
fhould

should Messiah be born?" they replied unanimously, "In Bethlehem of Jewdea; for thus it is written by the prophet. Thou, Bethlehem in the land of Jewdah—out of thee shall come the GOVERNOR that shall RULE my people ISRAEL," not Jewdah only, Matt. ii. 4—6. Micah v. 2. Hence then I conclude, that the thing intended in the patriarchal prediction is THE SPIRITUAL SCEPTER, the great "blessing of all men, promised to Abraham, established with Isaac, made to rest upon the head of Jacob *," and now fixed by Jacob in the tribe of Jewdah. And there it remained till Shiloh came. But when the Jews refused to submit to it, it departed from them to the Gentiles. "The kingdom of God, says our Saviour, shall be taken away from you, and given to a nation bringing forth the fruits thereof." This is THE SCEPTER OF JEWDAH. The very same scepter that was taken from the Jews was given to the Gentiles. And therefore it was a spiritual scepter, for the kingdom of Jesus is not of this world. So that this celebrated prediction is not, what it is commonly supposed to be, a promise of the continuance of the CIVIL scepter in the tribe of Jewdah till the Messiah came (which is false in fact) but a declaration of the departure of the SPIRITUAL scepter when he came.——I would just observe farther, that the supposition of a temporal scepter being the object of this prophecy is absolutely inconsistent with an express law of Moses. "When thou art come unto the land which the Lord thy God giveth thee, and shalt possess it, and shalt dwell therein, and shalt say, I will set a KING over me, like as all the nations that are about me, thou shalt in any wise set him king over thee, whom the Lord thy God shall choose; one FROM AMONG

THY

* Ecclus. xliv. 21—23.

THY BRETHREN fhalt thou fet KING over thee, thou mayft not fet a ftranger over thee, one which is not thy brother," Deut. xvii. 14, 15. Here, you fee, any Ifraelite, of any tribe, was eligible to the regal office. Accordingly, the firft who " prevailed above his bre- thren," in a civil fenfe, was BENJAMIN, and the laft was LEVI, for Herod was of no tribe.

[30] As this part of the vifion alludes to the cuftom of a king's affociating the prince royal into the fove- reignty with himfelf, I have afcribed to the perfonage, here intended, his proper charaƈter, for though he ap- peared " like a fon of man," he was in truth THE SON OF GOD. The Jews themfelves have gone before me in giving him this charaƈter, and Jefus accepts it. When he faid to the Jewifh council, " Hereafter fhall THE SON OF MAN fit on the right hand of the power of God," they all joined in this contemptuous queftion —— ART THOU THEN THE SON OF GOD? And he faid unto them, Ye fay that I AM." Luke xxii. 69, 70.

[31] Οι μιν γαρ ΜΟΝΑΡΧΙΑΙΣ, οι δι ταις ΟΛΙΓΩΝ δυναςκαις, αλλοι δι τοις ΠΛΗΘΕΣΙΝ ιπιτριψαν την ιξουσιαν των πολιτιυματων. Ο δι ημιτιρ⊙ νομοθιτης εις μιν τουτων ουδοτιων απωδιν (ως δ' αυτις ειποι βιασαμιν⊙ τον λογον). ΘΕΟΚΡΑΤΙΑΝ απιδειξι το πολιτιυμα, ΘΕΩ την αρχην κ̩ το κρατ⊙ αναθεις, κ. τ. λ. Contra Apion. lib. 2. §. 16. p. 1376. l. 37—42. Edit. Hudfon. This peculiar form of government fubfifted, as I have faid, from Mofes to Vefpafian. It is indeed commonly fuppofed, that the theocracy ceafed with the judges. But why then is SAUL ftyled, by David, " THE LORD's ANOINTED?" " THIS, as Bifhop Warburton obferves, was the common

mon title of the kings of Israel and Jewdah, and plainly
denoted their office of VICE-ROYALTY; improperly,
and superstitiously transferred, in these latter ages, to
CHRISTIAN kings and princes *." DAVID too was, in
this sense, " the Lord's anointed." " SOLOMON sat on
THE THRONE OF THE LORD, AS KING, instead of
David his father." But how could he sit upon THE
THRONE OF GOD, if the THEOCRACY HAD CEASED?
The queen of Sheba expresses her idea of the Jewish
form of government, which had doubtless been conveyed to her by Solomon himself in this handsome com-
pliment to him. " Blessed be THE LORD THY GOD,
which delighted in thee to set thee on HIS THRONE
to be KING FOR THE LORD THY GOD." " During
the captivity the theocracy lay, as it were, in abeyance.
But it was afterwards revived. " ACCORDING TO THE
WORD THAT I COVENANTED WITH YOU WHEN YOU
CAME OUT OF EGYPT, SO MY SPIRIT REMAINETH
AMONG YOU." What was THAT COVENANT? says
Bishop Warburton. That Israel should be his people,
and He their God and KING.—The meaning therefore
must be, That he would still continue their KING as
well as God †." Accordingly CYRUS is expresly styled,
by anticipation, " THE LORD'S SHEPHERD" and " THE
LORD'S ANOINTED," that is, his vice-roy in Jewdea.
Hence St Paul calls the Roman emperor " THE MINIS-
TER OF GOD," for Jerusalem was still " the holy city,
the city of THE GREAT KING;" and consequently
Cæsar, how supreme soever elsewhere, was, in Jewdea,
neither more nor less than PRO-IMPERATOR, GOD'S
LIEUTENANT; and therefore when the theocracy
ceased,

---

* Div. Leg. Vol. IV. p. 226.
† Ibid. p. 239—242.

ceafed, Cæfar's vice-royalty ceafed too. But as this interpretation may be thought fingular, and as' the apoftle's words have been twifted by party-writers, for different purpofes, to different fenfes, it may not be improper to fay fomething in fupport of it.

Let it be obferved then, that the Jews were poffeffed. of a notion of the unlawfulnefs of paying tribute, or any other kind of civil obedience, to a Pagan magif-trate, becaufe God alone was their lord and king.— This was the common principle of the nation, and it was publicly inculcated by Judas of Galilee in the days of the taxing under Cyrenius. He taught his countrymen, as Jofephus informs us, that they muft be downright cowards, ει φορον τε Ρωμαιοις τελειν υπομινωσι, κ) ΜΕΤΑ ΤΟΝ ΘΕΟΝ οισωσι ΘΝΗΤΟΥΣ δισποτας, if they could fubmit both to pay tribute to the Romans, and TOGETHER WITH God acknowledge mortal (that is, heathen) Lords." J. W. b. ii. c. 8. § 1. I tranflate μετα τον Θεον (not after, but) together with God, becaufe we learn from the fame Jofephus, that the followers of Judas acknowledged GOD to be their ONLY governor and king, and called no MAN (that is, no heathen) their LORD." Ant. b. xviii. c. 1. §. 6. The fame principles dictated thofe infnaring queftions to Jefus, " Is it LAWFUL [for Jews] to give tribute to CÆSAR, or NOT [lawful]? Shall we give? or fhall we not give?" Mark xii. 14, 15. Jefus admits fo much of the firft principle as was true *, and thereby over-turns the fecond, which was falfe. " WHOSE is this image and fuperfcription," fays he, upon the tribute money? They fay, Cæfar's. He replies, " Render therefore

* Namely, that God was at that time their king and governor.

therefore to Cæfar the things that are Cæfar's, and to God the things that are God's." ver. 16, 17. As if he had faid, You boaft of being fubjects of the theocracy. But from Mofes' time to this the theocracy has been adminiftered by a deputy. Now God's deputy muft be of God's appointing. And Cæfar's image and fuperfcription, which you acknowledge to be upon the current money of Jewdea, are plain tokens that Cæfar is deputy. " Render therefore to Cæfar the things that are Cæfar's, and to God the things that are God's;" or, in other words, Fear God, and honor his king.

This is the true ground of St Paul's reafoning in his epiftle to the Romans. Too many JEWISH converts ftill retained a fcrupulous attachment to the law of Mofes, and, among other prejudices, thofe I have already mentioned. Many of the converts from GENTILISM, mifled by " thofe of the circumcifion," embraced the fame notions, and JEWDAISED too. To both thefe parties, very numerous at Rome, the apoftle thus addreffes himfelf. " Let EVERY (Chriftian) foul be fubject to the fupreme powers, for there is no power but of God; the powers that be, ΥΠΟ του Θεου τεταγμεναι εισιν, are appointed BY and UNDER God." Saul was appointed by and under God as well as David, Jeroboam as well as Solomon, Cyrus and Alexander had the fame divine appointment, and Cæfar, the then prefent power, had the fame. This the Jews well knew. And therefore our Saviour exprefsly charges them with HYPOCRISY, in the queftion concerning the LAWFULNESS of paying tribute to the Roman emperor. " Whofoever therefore refifteth the power, refifteth the ordinance of God; and they that refift fhall receive to themfelves damnation," that is, temporal deftruction, as the Jewifh

people

people did under Vefpafian. I underſtand the word
κριμα in a temporal fenfe, becaufe it plainly ſtands oppofed to ϲωτηρια, a temporal " falvation," in the eleventh verfe. " Now, fays the apoſtle, is OUR SAL-
VATION NEARER than when we (firſt) believed;"
a falvation, not at the laſt judgment, but in that
" day of vifitation," Luke xix. 44.—1Pet. ii. 12. which
was to bring deſtruction to the Jews, and a deliverance
to the Chriſtians from the Jewiſh powers. The deſtruction of Jerufalem was then nigh at hand, and therefore the day of falvation to the Chriſtians was nigh at
hand too—it was nearer than when they firſt believed.
But what were the few years from their converſion to
the many centuries before the day of Judgment? The
apoſtle goes on thus. " Now † rulers are not a terror
to good works, but to the evil. Wilt thou then not
be afraid of the power? Do that which is good, and
thou ſhalt have praife of the fame (power), for he is
the miniſter of God to thee for good. But if thou do
that which is evil, be afraid; for he beareth not the
fword in vain, for he is the revenging miniſter of God
for wrath to him that doeth evil. Wherefore ye muſt
needs be fubject, not only for wrath (that will be executed by Cæfar), but alfo for confcience (towards God
whofe vicegerent he is). Now † for the fame caufe
pay tribute alfo, for they are the Miniſters of God, per-
fevering * in this very thing. Render therefore |to all
their dues; tribute, to whom tribute (is due); cuſtom,
to whom cuſtom; fear, to whom fear; honor, to whom

K   honor."

† The facred, as well as other Greek writers, frequently
begin a fentence with γαρ, as we do with NOW.

* The word προϲκαρτεϱϋντιϲ does not relate to the
POWERS but to the SUBJECTS.

honor." Rom. xiii. 1—7. I fhall leave this fubject, as
Bifhop Sherlock does, "without drawing any confe-
quences, excepting one only, namely, That the fcriptures are not to be tortured to fpeak in favor of one fide
or another; for they ftand clear of all difputes about the
rights of princes and fubjects; fo that fuch difputes muft
be left to be decided by principles of natural equity and
the conftitutions of the country." Vol. IV. p. 371.

[32] The verb tranfitive is often ufed imperfonally.
" In that day fhall ONE take up a parable againft you;"
Mic. ii. 4. literally, he fhall take up. " One " is
here fupplied by the tranflators, as it is elfewhere. So,
that the place may be rendered, agreeably to the vulgar Latin, " There SHALL BE TAKEN UP a parable."
In like manner the Hebrew mode of expreffion, " HE
SHALL CALL his name Wonderful," is very properly
changed in our verfion, which fays, " His name SHALL
BE CALLED Wonderful." Ifai. ix. 6. The circumftances in Daniel's vifion are defcribed as they happened.
1. A beaft with ten horns. 2. Another horn. 3. Three
of the ten fall, that is, " WERE PLUCKED UP," as
Daniel himfelf expreffes it. How they were plucked
up is not faid, nor was there any occafion to fay it.
For what could break off the horns of this beaft, but
the beaft itfelf?

[33] For the ufe of the term falvation in a temporal
fenfe, fee Dr Hammond in various places of his para-
phrafe and annotations; and for the fact, that the believing Jews were faved, in this fenfe of the expreffion,
fee Eufebius in his Ecclefiaftical hiftory. b. 3. c. 5. Our
Saviour himfelf foretold it. " When thefe things [falfe
Chrifts, wars and commotions, the encompaffing of Jerufalem

rufalem with armies, &c.] begin to come to pafs, then look up and lift your heads, for YOUR REDEMPTION draweth nigh." Luke xxi. 28. Jofephus ufes the word σωτήρια, on this occafion, in the fame fenfe. See J.W. b. III. c. VII. §. 5.

[34] This was not a wanton fally of refentment from the injured prifoner, but a calm and folemn, though dreadful, denunciation of the infpired apoftle. Τυπτειν σε μιλλει ὁ Θεὸς. St Paul addreffes the high prieft as the reprefentative of the Jewifh nation. He had open-ed his fpeech to the council in this manner. " Bre-thren, I have lived in all good confcience towards God until this day." The high prieft was offended, and " commanded them that ftood by Paul to fmite him on the mouth." The apoftle replies, "God will fmite thee, thou whited wall." This gave frefh offence, and fome of the ftanders-by faid, " Revileft thou God's high prieft? for it is written, Thou fhalt not fpeak evil of the RULER of thy people." This quotation from the law is commonly fuppofed to be part of St Paul's anfwer to the accufation, and to contain a kind of apology for his reflection on the high prieft, not knowing him to be fo. But this cannot be admitted. St Paul was certainly included in the general promife to the apoftles. " They will lay their hands on you, and perfecute you, deliver-ing you up to the fynagogues, and into prifons, being brought before kings and rulers for my name's fake.— Settle it therefore in your hearts, not to meditate before what ye fhall anfwer ; for I will give you a mouth and wifdom, which all your adverfaries fhall not be able to gainfay, nor refift;" Luke xxi. 12—15. or, as it is exprefled in St Mark, " whatfoever fhall be given you

in

in that hour, that fpeak ye; for it is not ye that fpeak,
but the Holy Ghoft." xiii. 11. Now will you fay, that
the Holy Ghoft is here making apologies? Or can you
ferioufly believe, that Paul, "brought up in Jerufalem
at the feet of Gamaliel," did not know the high prieft?
If he did not know the man, he muft have known the
magiftrate, by his habit, and by his place in the council, which Paul "beheld earneftly." And, accordingly
he addreffes him as fuch. "Sitteft thou to JUDGE me
after the law?" Where then is the pertinence of the
quotation, as coming from St Paul? The apoftle could
fay nothing that required an apology. And therefore
when he was charged with having "reviled God's high
prieft," he replies roundly, Oυκ ηδειν, "I do not acknowledge that he is high-prieft," that is, "God's high-prieft"
the high-prieft mentioned by the objector. Nor was
he fo. He held his office, not according to the law of
Mofes, but by the appointment of the Roman governor;
he was an "ungodly wretch, and NOT HIGH-PRIEST,"
as Jafon who had a fimilar appointment, is defcribed
in the fecond book of Maccabees, iv. 13. Place then
St Paul's words in a parenthefis, and connect the quotation with the objector's queftion, to which it belongs,
and with which only it has a proper agreement. "Revileft thou God's high-prieft? (and Paul faid, I do not
acknowledge, brethren, that he is high-prieft) for it
is written, thou fhalt not fpeak evil of the ruler of thy
people." St Luke himfelf has a paffage exactly parallel
to this conftruction. "And he faid unto them that
ftood by, Take from him the pound, and give it to him
that hath ten pounds; (and they faid unto him, Lord,
he hath ten pounds) for I fay unto you, that unto every
one which hath fhall be given, and from him that hath
not, even that he hath fhall be taken away from him."
chap. xix. 22—26.

[35] Which

{35} " Which of the prophets have not your fathers perfecuted? and they have flain them which fhewed before of the coming of the JUST ONE, of whom ye have been now the betrayers and murderers." Acts vii. 52.

[36] The CHRONOLOGY of the JEWISH WAR, from Jofephus.

The Jewifh war began in the month Artemifius *, in the TWELFTH year of NERO.

In HYPERBERETEUS Ceftius brought his army before the city.

Without any reafonable caufe he leaves it.

Is defeated by the Jews on the 8th day of DIUS, in the TWELFTH year of NERO.

Vefpafian is employed by Nero againft the Jews.

Titus failed from Achaia to Alexandria fooner than the WINTER feafon did ufually permit.

K 3   Vefpafian,

* The Macedonian months, here ufed, anfwer to the Jewifh, as appears from Jofephus himfelf, who fays, that " the pafsover was on the fourteenth day of Xanthicus," confefsedly Nifan, or the firft month. He fays too, that " the fecond temple was burnt on the tenth day of Lous, the fame day on which the firft had been burnt," that is, the month Ab, or " the fifth month " according to Jeremiah. LII. 12. The months then will ftand thus.

1. Nifan.	Xanthicus.
2. Jiar.	Artemifius.
3. Sivan.	Dæfius.
4. Tamuz.	Panemus.
5. Ab.	Lous.
6. Elul.	Gorpieus.
7. Tifri.	Hyperbereteus.
8. Marchefvan.	Dius.
9. Cafleu.	Apelleus.
10. Tabeth.	Audineus.
11. Schebath.	Peritius.
12. Adar.	Dyftrus.

Vefpafian, willing to demolifh Jotapata, was prevented by Jofephus, the 21ˢᵗ of ARTEMISIUS.

A terrible fight there between the Jews and Romans, the 20ᵗʰ of DESIUS.

Another at Japha, the 25ᵗʰ.

Another at Gerizim between the Romans and Samaritans, the 27th.

Jotapata taken, the 1ft of PANÉMUS in the THIRTEENTH of NERO.

Jofephus taken prifoner there.

The inhabitants of Taricheæ made prifoners, the 8th of GORPIEUS.

The Romans enter Gamala, the 23ᵈ of HYPERBERETEUS.

Vefpafian enters Gadara, the 4th of DYSTRUS.

———— encamps at Neapolis, the 2ᵈ of DESIUS.

———— went the next day to Jericho.

———— is informed that Nero is dead, having reigned 13 years and eight days.

GALBA made emperor—flain in the market-houfe at Rome, having reigned 7 months and feven days.

OTHO made emperor—kills himfelf after reigning three months and two days.

VITELLIUS made emperor.

Vefpafian removed from Cæfarea the 5th of DESIUS.

Simon gets Poffeffion of Jerufalem in XANTHICUS, in the third year of the war.

VESPASIAN made emperor in the eaft.

VITELLIUS flain in Apelleus, having reigned eight months and five days.

On the 15th day of the fiege of Jerufalem, the 7th of ARTEMISIUS, Titus got poffeffion of the firft wall.

The fecond wall taken the fifth day after taking the firft.

Titus

Titus was willing to preferve the city for his own fake, and the temple for the fake of the city.

The Romans are forced to quit the city. The Jews elated with their fuccefs, imagine that the Romans will not come there again, and that they fhall not be conquered, if they renew the battle; for G o d, fays Jofephus, had BLINDED THEIR MINDS for their tranfgreffions *.

The fourth day after Titus recovers the wall.

He intermits the fiege four days, and renews it on the fifth.

The Romans began to raife their banks the 12th of ARTEMISIUS, and finifhed them by the 29th.

The tower of Antonia taken.

On the 22d of PANEMUS the Jews themfelves fet fire to the N. W. cloifter of the temple.

Two days after the Romans fet fire to the adjoining cloifter.

The famine was fo great in the city, that a noble lady killed her own fon, a child fucking at her breaft,

K 4

then

---

* Jofephus fays B. v. c. 13. §. 5. ΘΕΟΣ δε ην ο του λαου ΠΑΝΤΟΣ ΚΑΤΑΚΡΙΝΑΣ, κ) πασαν αυτοις ΣΩΤΗΡΙΑΣ οδον εις απωλειαν αποςρεφων. " It was God that had CONDEMNED the WHOLE people, and turned every way for their SAFETY to their DESTRUCTION." This paffage, added to that above is in part a comment upon what St Paul fays to the Theffalonians. Δια τουτο πεμψει αυτοις Ὁ ΘΕΟΣ ΕΝΕΡΓΕΙΑΝ ΠΛΑΝΗΣ, εις το πιςευσαι αυτους τω ψευδει. ινα ΚΡΙΘΩΣΙ ΠΑΝΤΕΣ οι μη πιςευσαιτες τη αληθεια. " For this caufe G o d fhall fend them ftrong DELUSION, that they may believe a lie, that they ALL may be CONDEMNED who believe not the truth." 2 Theff. ii. 11, 12.

then roasted him, and ate one part of him, referving the other for a future meal *.

On the 8th of Lous Titus placed the battering rams against the western part of the inner temple.

On the 10th, that fatal day of Lous, upon which the temple had been formerly burnt by the Babylonians, it was again burnt down in the SECOND year of VESPA-SIAN.

Banks are raifed againft the upper city, the 20th of Lous.

———— finifhed the 7th of Gorpieus.

Jerufalem burnt and taken the 8th.

See Ptolemy's canon in note [48].

[37] So Rev. v. 5. our Saviour is ftyled the LION of the tribe of Jewdah, and yet immediately appears as a LAMB that had been flain.

[39] Job xxxix. 30. " Where the flain are, there is fhe," the eagle. Hence fome learned writers have been led to conclude, that our Saviour's expreffion is, only, PROVERBIAL. But why may not a PROVERB, ufed PROPHETICALLY, have a LITERAL fignification ? " If the reader calls to mind the PREDICTION of our Lord, as it is elfewhere expreffed without a figure— When ye fhall fee Jerufalem compaffed with ARMIES " Luke xxi. 20. and compares it with the EVENT, he will hardly make a doubt whether EAGLES, in thofe
figurative

* Well might our Saviour fay to the " daughters of Jeru-falem, Weep not for me, but weep for yourfelves and for your children. For behold ! the days are coming, in the which they fhall fay, BLESSED ARE THE BARREN, and THE WOMBS THAT NEVER BARE, AND THE PAPS WHICH NEVER GAVE SUCK." Luke XXIII. 28, 29.

figurative predictions, which respect the same subject, namely, the destruction of Jerusalem, were not intended by our Lord to denote the ROMAN armies." Dr Hurd's Lectures p. 167. n. I am happy in having the suffrage of this eminent critic.

[40] "Sicut ANTICÆSAREM dicimus QUI contra Cæsarem SE CÆSAREM VULT DICI ATQUE CÆSAR HABERI, sic ANTICHRISTUS est qui se vero Christo opponit EO MODO ut ipse Christus haberi velit." Grotius, append. de Antichristo, p. . The eminent critic, above mentioned, has lately controverted this opinion of the excellent Grotius. " The learned commentator did not reflect, that words are not always used according to the strict import of their etymologies. FALSE CHRISTS, we will say, are, in the strict sense of the word ANTICHRISTS. But the question is, in WHAT sense this word is used of the person called, by way of eminence, THE ANTICHRIST?—Besides, it is not so clear, as Grotius supposes, that the strict sense of the word, ANTICHRISTUS, must be—is, qui se vero Christo opponit, eo modo ut ipse Christus haberi velit. Cæsar, who generally expressed himself with exact propriety, thought fit, on a certain occasion, to assume the name and character of ANTICATO. Was it Cæsar's purpose to say, or was it his ambition to pretend, " That he opposed himself to the true Cato, EO MODO ut ipse CATO haberi vellet ?" Lect. p. 217, 218. n.

It is with the greatest regret, that I find myself obliged to dissent from this ingenious, learned, and fashionable writer, especially in his proper province of CRITICISM. But here he seems to be mistaken in every point. Grotius was so far from not reflecting, that words are not always used according to their strict import,

port, that his reasoning is founded on that very reflection. CÆSAR, he well knew, from being a FAMILY
name, became a name of OFFICE and DIGNITY. Tacitus, speaking of the Jewish aversion to images, says,
"Non REGIBUS hæc adulatio, non CÆSARIBUS honor," that is, the Jews would not allow such a com-
pliment either to KINGS or EMPERORS. Hiſtor. B. v.
f. 5. Accordingly Grotius having mentioned the family
of the Cæsars says, "Cæsares JAM voco eos qui NATU-
RA aut ADOPTIONE ad Cæsarum DOMUM pertinebant,
quales ante Galbam omnes," (Ibid. p. 55.) plainly im-
plying, that he elsewhere used the word, Cæsar, in a
different sense. Indeed the passage itself, quoted by Dr
Hurd, is a sufficient proof of it. The terms CHRIST
and CÆSAR are evidently used as names of OFFICE, and
therefore ANTICHRIST and ANTICÆSAR must be used
so too. Nor did Grotius, as the Doctor would insi-
nuate, fetch his meaning of Antichrist from the ety-
mology, but from the use, of the term. "CHRIST
HIMSELF, according to Dr Hurd, had made the appearance of FALSE CHRISTS and false prophets, that
is, of ANTICHRISTS, to be one of the SIGNS by which
that HOUR (mentioned by St John, and so fatal to the
Jews) should be distinguished." p. 214. This is indeed
the truth. "Many, says our Saviour, shall come IN
MY NAME, saying, I AM THE CHRIST." Matt. xxiv. 5.
"NOMEN sæpe OFFICIUM aut DIGNITATEM alicujus
significat. Dicuntur ergo hîc exstituri qui sibi ascribant
dignitatem eam quæ Jesu est propria, i. e. ut sequitur,
QUI SE DICTURI SUNT CHRISTOS. CHRISTI nomine
populus Judaicus intelligebat vindicem libertatis. Nam
illud, ἡμεις δι ηλπιζομεν οτι αυτ⊕ ιςιν ὁ μελλων λυτρουσαι
τον Ισραηλ, Luc. xxiv. 41. descriptio est nominis CHRIS-
TI. Quare quicunque se missos divinitus liberatores
populi

populi Judaici dicebant, eo ipfo CHRISTOS SE profi-
tebantur, et erant ψευδοχριτοι." Grot. in loc. Thefe
predictions, then current in the church, are clearly
alluded to by St John, when he fays, "Ye have HEARED
that ANTICHRIST fhall come." 1 Ep. ii. 18. The apoftle had faid, "IT IS THE LAST TIME," of the Jewifh
church and ftate, or, in other words, it IS the LAST
of Daniel's SEVENTY WEEKS. In fupport of his affer-
tion he appeals to fome noted predictions, that " ANTI-
CHRIST SHOULD COME" IN THE LAST TIME, for
fo the ellipfis muft be fupplied. " Little children, it
is the LAST time; and as ye have heared, THAT ANTI-
CHRIST SHALL COME" at THAT time, "fo NOW there
are many Antichrifts: whereby we know that it IS the
LAST time." The apoftle is not fpeaking of fome future Antichrift, but of fuch as really exifted at that
very time. Here is no MORALIZING, but ftrict, fober REASONING. Antichrift was to appear in the laft
time of the Jewifh ftate. Many Antichrifts appeared
in St John's time. THEREFORE, fays he, it is the
laft time.—And now, I think, it will appear, that
the Doctor's ANTICATO is by no means a parallel
with Antichrift. Cato fignified only the name of a
perfon. Confequently Anticato could denote nothing
more than a perfonal oppofition. And even if Cato
had affumed the name of Anticæfar, it could have denoted nothing more. But CHRIST was always a name
of OFFICE; and therefore ANTICHRIST muft be too.
Many will come in my name, faying, I AM CHRIST."

[41] Rev. ii. 9. and iii. 9. This indeed is faid of the
Churches of SMYRNA and SARDIS, Jews, in this
prophetic book, ftanding for Chriftians. But then what
is here faid muft firft have been true of the Jews in the
literal

literal fenfe, before it could be applied to thofe Anti-
chriftian churches in the fpiritual.   Juft as papal ROME
could not have been ftyled, in the fame prophetic book,
BABYLON the great, if Babylon had not before been
" the mother of harlots and abominations of the earth."
chap. xvii. 5.

[42] " He caufeth——that no man might buy or
fell, fave he that had the MARK or the NAME of the
BEAST, or the NUMBER OF HIS NAME. Here is wifdom.
Let him that hath underftanding count the NUMBER
OF THE BEAST.   Now it is the number of a MAN.
And his number is fix hundred fixty and fix." Rev.
xiii. 17, 18.   " Here, fays Father Calmet, the CURI-
OUS are PERPLEXED—there are many CONJECTURES
on this matter, and almoft all the commentators have
TRIED their abilities, without being able to fay certainly that any of them have fucceeded, in giving us
the true MARK of the BEAST, or the CYPHER whereby
he will DISTINGUISH his followers.—He therefore advifes us, as the WISEST and the SAFEST way, to be
SILENT with refpect to both this NAME and CHARAC-
TER."   [Dictionary, under the word ANTICHRIST.]
Well faid ! Pere Calmet ; for no one, acquainted with
the name and character of the beaft, will be a member
of the church of Rome.   But " let him that hath underftanding count the number of the beaft," that he
may know and avoid him.   The following remarks
may, perhaps, lead us to a difcovery of his name.

1. A beaft is the fymbol of a ftate.

2. The number of the beaft is the number of his
name, that is, the numerical value of the letters in his
name is equal to 666, the number given.

3. This

3. This number is the number of a man. As every number is the number of a man, the term man muft here be ufed in fome peculiar fenfe. Now the Jews call Gentiles by the name of men. So Zech. ix. 1. "the eyes of MAN, as of all the tribes of ISRAEL, fhall be towards the Lord." Matt. xvii. 22. " The Son of man fhall be delivered into the hands of men," the Gentiles. St Peter ufes the word ανθρωπιν⊕ in the fame fenfe. " Submit yourfelves to every HUMAN creature," to every Gentile, to whom fubmiffion is due; the emperor, governors, hufbands and mafters, 1 Ep. ii. 13. Judas the Galilean, as we have feen in note [31], perfuaded his followers, that it was unlaw-ful for a Jew to acknowledge any MAN, that is, any Heathen, as his lord and governor, for they fubmitted to the government of their own countrymen. Jofephus has another remarkable paffage. I will fet it down in the original, that the reader may judge, whether Zabulon or Galilee is called the place of MEN. Ωρμησιν [Κιστ⊕] επι πολιν καρτεραν της Γαλιλαι⊕ Ζαβυλων, η καλειται ΑΝΔΡΩΝ. J. W. b. ii. c. 18. f. 9. The fcripture ex-preffion is, Γαλιλαια των εθνων, "Galilee of the Gentiles." Ifai. ix. 1.=Matt. iv. 15. According to this fenfe, the name, and confequently the number of the name, muft be in GREEK letters.

4. Kings are ufed for kingdoms. The fourth king, or empire, was the Roman. Ρωμαι⊕ therefore was the name of the fourth beaft. Now when St John faw thefe vifions the Roman was one intire empire. But the fpirit of prophecy forefaw the time when this empire, foon after its converfion to the faith of Chrift, would be divided into two parts——civilly, into the eaftern and weftern empires; ecclefiaftically, into the Greek and Latin churches. Where then are we to look for
this

this new edition of the Roman beast? in the east or in the west? at Conftantinople or at Rome? and what is his name? " Here is wifdom," fays the angel; and the man of wifdom, " he that hath underftanding," will follow the advice of the angel, and " count the number of the beaft;" for his number will fhew his name, and his name will lead us to his ftation.

The name of the old Roman beaft, or Pagan Rome, was, as I have faid, Ρωμαιθ. But this name does not contain the number. Befides, this name was common to both empires. The emperors were alike ftyled RoMAN, and their fubjects ROMANS. Conftantinople was called NEW ROME, and the country about it RoMANIA. And it may be obferved too, that New, as well as Old, Rome is feated on feven hills.

The fuccefs of our inquiry will therefore depend upon our finding out that fpecific NAME of a kingdom (whatever it is, and wherever it is) the NUMBER of which will at once difcriminate both the beaft and his followers.

Now IRENÆUS, a very antient ecclefiaftical writer, who knew nothing of the divifion of the empire into eaftern and weftern, Greek and Latin, has, among other traditions, tranfmitted down to us the name Λατινθ as containing the number of this queftionable beaft. This deferves our attention; for the FACT is, that, after the divifion of the empire, the fubfcriptions of the eaftern and weftern Bifhops, in their general councils, were made under the diftinct fpecific titles of GREEK fathers and LATIN fathers.

Count then the NUMBER of the NAME

$$\Lambda \quad A \quad T \quad \Sigma \quad I \quad N \quad O \quad \Sigma$$
$$30 + 1 + 300 + 5 + 10 + 50 + 70 + 200$$

and you will find it $= 666$.

And

And as Λατεινος* is the NAME of the BEAST, and
contains the NUMBER of the NAME, so does it include
his MARK likewise. LATIN is the CHARACTERISTIC
of the PAPAL church. She LATINIZES in every thing.
Are not all her trumpery, BULLS, CANONS, COUNCILS,
DECRETALS, in LATIN ? Are not all her solemnities
too, BIBLE, CREED, MASS, HYMNS, LITANY, in
LATIN ? Nay, do not even the Greek ejaculations,
adopted by her, bear the same MARK, and appear in
LATIN characters ?—Kyrie eleeson—Chrifte eleeson—
LATIN then is the one difcriminating MARK of the
POPE's KINGDOM ; the SIBBOLETH of the ROMAN-
CATHOLIC CHURCH. We may therefore apply to
every fubject of Peter's fucceffor what was faid to Peter
himfelf, " Surely thou art a GALILEAN, for thy
SPEECH bewrayeth thee." And we need not fcruple
to fix the SEAT of the apocalyptic BEAST at ROME
in ITALY.

True

* Grotius excepts againft the orthography of Λατεινος, as
if it ought to be written Λατινος. But the authority of old
ENNIUS may fairly be put in the fcale againft that of any
modern critic. Take then the following inftances in one,
expreffion—Popolei tenuere Lateinei. Dr More has
collected many other inftances out of the fame writer, but
thefe are fufficient to fhew, efpecially as one is a cafe
in point, that the Latins ufed the diphthong for i long.
Ireneus too exhibits the name in the fame form. And,
poffibly the tradition came from St John himfelf, who
might have feen upon the forehead of the BEAST—

MYΣTHPION,
ΛATEINOΣ.
χ ξ ς.

Let the Reader read from the 11th verfe to the end of the
chapter, and judge of this. St John feems to me to have
feen what he wrote.

True it is, as the induſtry of the Popiſh writers has fully proved, that the NUMBER may be found in many other NAMES. But then it is equally true, that thoſe names are nothing to the purpoſe. According to the analogy of interpreting ſymbolic prophecies, as the BEAST is a KINGDOM, the NAME of the BEAST muſt be the NAME of a KINGDOM. To what purpoſe then is it, to amuſe us with the PERSONAL names, ULPIUS*, Mohamed †, Luther ‡, and perhaps a thouſand others, if

* ΟΥΛΠΙΟΣ. Here they are forced to ſink the value of Σ 200 to that of ς, which ſignifies the number 6.

† ΜΟΑΜΕΤΙΣ.

‡ לולתל as they chooſe to give us the name.

The only name in Calmet's catalogue that comes near the truth is רומייח (Romana). The numeral value of theſe letters is exactly 666. This is the name adopted by Mr DAUBUZ, the celebrated commentator on the Revelation. But, with great ſubmiſſion to ſo able a judge of theſe matters, it is only near the truth. The number 666 expreſſed in HEBREW letters is not the number of a MAN. St John, ſpeaking of another KING, informs us, that " his NAME in the HEBREW tongue is ABADDON, but in the GREEK tongue APOLLYON;" or, in other words, his name is ABADDON in the JEWS' language, but APOLLYON in that of a MAN. Rev. ix. 11. But the great objection to רומייח is its gender. The name ſhould be in agreement with KING, according to the prophetic uſe of king for kingdom. " The four BEASTS are four KINGS." Dan. vii. 17. And Daniel ſays to the KING of BABYLON, " THOU art the head of gold." ii. 38. The NAME therefore of the fourth BEAST, the ſymbol of the fourth KING, muſt be Ρωμαιος, not Ρωμαια, nor רומייח in the Hebrew. Not to mention, that there would have been no great WISDOM in diſcovering that the NAME of the fourth empire was ROMAN, which, however, in the preſent caſe, would be no name of diſtinction.

i
f indeed they contained the number, but to fhew us their dexterity in the arts of controverfy, and their readinefs to trifle with ferious fubjects.

[43] So the paffage is applied even by Grotius. " Admonitio Pauli Rom. xi. 22. proprie quidem Romanis accommodata eft, quos plane velim ejus femper meminiffe." Append. de Antic. p. 84.

[44] This expreffion, confidered by itfelf, may fignify "thine own fake." But here "the LORD" feems evidently oppofed to "the SERVANT" in the eleventh verfe, and therefore MESSIAH feems to be the oppofite of MOSES. St Paul has a fimilar fentiment: "Mofes was faithful—as a fervant, but Chrift as a fon." Heb. iii. 5, 6.

[45] St Paul had faid to the converted Jews of Theffalonica, in his firft epiftle, " Ye, brethren, became followers of the churches of God which in Jewdea are in Chrift Jefus; for ye alfo have fuffered like things of your own countrymen (the ignoble Jews of Theffalonica) even as they have of the Jews (in Jewdea); who both killed the Lord Jefus and their own prophets, and have perfecuted us (the apoftles); and they pleafe not God, and are contrary to all men—to fill up their fins alway; for WRATH IS COME UPON THEM ας τιλθ, AT THE END." Chap. ii. 14—16. From this, and other paffages to the fame purpofe, mifunderftood by the "unlearned," and perverted by the "unftable," the afflicted Chriftians were feduced into a miftaken opinion, that the day of their deliverance from the

L   Jewifh

Jewish perfecutors, by the deftruction of Jerufalem,
" was at hand." To correct this fatal error is one
part of the apoftle's defign in his fecond epiftle. "Now
we befeech you, brethren, concerning the coming of
our Lord Jefus Chrift, and our gathering together *
unto him, that ye be not foon fhaken from your (former) opinion, nor be troubled †, either by fpirit, (any
falfe teacher,) or by word or by letter, as from us (the
apoftles of Chrift) as that the day of Chrift ('s firft coming to judgment) is at hand. Let no man deceive you
by any means. For (that day will not come) except
there firft be the falling away ‡ (of the Jewifh nation
from the Roman government) that § the man of fin
may be revealed, the fon of perdition, who (now) op-
pofeth (the Romans) and exalteth himfelf above every
one called God or Worfhip ‖ (Divus or Auguftus) fo
that he as God (or king) fitteth (or ruleth) in the
temple ¶ of God (the king) fhewing himfelf that he
is

* "The gathering together", fpoken of by our Saviour.
Mat. xxiv. 31.

† The fame word, and on the fame occafion, Mat. xxiv. 6.

‡ Αποςασια. This noun and its verb are frequently ufed
By Jofephus to exprefs the Jewifh APOSTASY from the Roman government.

§ και is frequently ufed in this fenfe. See Mat. v. 15,
xxv. 27. Luke xv. 23.

¶ Σιβασμα in the abftract, by a very ufual Hebraifm, for
Σιβαςος.

¶ Here again I am fo unfortunate as to diffent from the
learned Dr HURD. " St Paul, prophefying of the Man
of fin, or Antichrift, to be revealed in the latter days,
makes

Is God (or king). Remember ye not, that when I was
yet with you I told you these things [the APOSTASY
and the REVELATION of the man of sin?] Και νυν
το κατεχον οιδατε, εις το αποκαλυφθηναι αυτον εν τω εαυτου
καιρω. The English version is, "And now ye know
what WITHHOLDETH that he might be revealed in his
time." And the usual comment is, that there was
some " LET or IMPEDIMENT to the coming of the
man of sin." But if there be any sense and meaning
in this tranflation or interpretation, I freely confess,
that I am not able to reach it. If a certain time had
been fixed in the decrees of Providence, for the manifeftation of this " man of sin," Who, or what could
have L E T and hindered it? There is evidently an
ellipfis, which may be fupplied in this manner. " Remember ye not, that when I was yet with you I told
you thefe things? So now know ye, that he who holdeth the temple will fall away from and oppofe the Ro-

L 2   mans,

makes it a diftinguifhing part of his character, ' That he
SITTETH IN THE TEMPLE OF GOD.' Confider the force of
thefe words. A power, ' feated in the temple of God,' CAN
BE NOTHING but a power fuitable to that place, or a SPIRI-
TUAL power; juft as a power, feated in the throne of Cæfar,
could only be interpreted of a civil power." p. 361. This
is, in Dr Hurd's idea, a graphical defcription of the POPE.
But what the Pope of ROME has to do in an epiftle to the
THESSALONIANS I know not. I am "no blancher of Popery," nor would I endeavour to fix a character upon the
Pope which does not appear to belong to him. If the temple here fpoken of was that at Jerufalem, the power feated
there was a civil power, for God was king of the Jews in
the fame fenfe as Cæfar was king of the Romans.

mans, that he may be revealed in his feafon." This man of fin was in being when St Paul wrote, but was not to be revealed till fome future time, his appointed feafon. "For the myftery of iniquity is already working." That is, the man of fin is even now at work, but fecretly. This we know to be the fact. Under the mafk of acknowledging "NO KING BUT CÆSAR," the Jews were meditating, at that very time, to wreft the fcepter out of Cæfar's hand, and to tranflate the feat of empire from Rome to Jerufalem. "Only he who now holdeth" the temple muft work on "till it be taken out of the way. And then fhall that wicked one be revealed." To underftand this we muft obferve, that the difpute between the Jews and Chriftians was, Which were the true church of God? If Chriftians, the followers of Jefus, were this true church, the Jews could be only pretenders to that character. But how was the difpute to be fettled? Alas! the Chriftians had nothing to fhew, on their behalf, but their MIRACLES, their SUFFERINGS, and their PATIENCE—poor evidences to "a perverfe and crooked generation," who had ftill their temple, the acknowledged token of the theocracy, ftanding vifibly among them; from whence they falfely concluded that, becaufe they were now the CIVIL, they were likewife the SPIRITUAL, kingdom of God. But the day of decifion was now approaching, when God would fhew "Who were His, and who were holy." The deftruction of the temple would be a full manifeftation of the man of fin feated there, "whom the Lord will confume with the fpirit of his mouth, and deftroy with the brightnefs of his coming. Even him, as the

apoftle

apoftle goes on to defcribe him, whofe coming is after the working of Satan, with all lying power, and figns, and wonders *, and with all deceivablenefs of unrighteoufnefs, in them that perifh, becaufe they received not the love of the truth, that they might be faved †. And for this caufe God will fend them ftrong delufions that they fhould believe a lie, that they all might be damned [in a temporal fenfe,] who believed not the truth, but had pleafure in unrighteoufnefs "—the juft judgment of thofe, who, having rejected the true Meffiah, liftened with pleafure to every profligate pretender to the character, 2 Thef. ii. 1—12.

[46] St Paul ufes the prepofition δια elfewhere in in the fame fenfe. Thus 2 Cor. ii. 4. ΔΙΑ πολλων δακρυων, " WITH many tears." Thus too Heb. ix. 12. Ουδι ΔΙ' αιματος τραγων και μοχων, ΔΙΑ δι του ιδιου αιματος — neither WITH the blood of goats and calves, but WITH his own blood he entered in once into the holy place, having obtained eternal redemption." Δια in this verfe is clearly the fame as ου χωρις, " not WITHOUT blood," in the feventh.

[47] Literally, " to return and build," that is, " to build again," as it is in the margin. So in the latter part of the verfe the fame phrafe is rightly rendered, " fhall be built again."

L 3

[48] An

---

[48]   An Extract from PTOLEMY's Canon.

	Years of K.	N,
		122
Nabopolaſſar - - - - - - -	21	143
Nabocolaſſar - - - - - - -	43	186
Ilvarodamus - - - - - - -	2	188
Niricaſſolaſſar - - - - - -	4	192
Nabonadius - - - - - - -	17	209
CYRUS - - - - - - -	9	218
Cambyſes - - - - - - -	8	226
Darius [Hyſtaſpis] - - - - -	36	262
Artaxerxes [Longimanus] - -	41	324
Darius II. [Nothus] - - - -	19	343
Artaxerxes II. [Mnemon] - -	46	389
Ochus - - - - - - -	21	410
Aroſtus - - - - - - -	2	412
Darius III. [Codomannus] - -	4	416
ALEXANDER - - - - - - -	8	424
Philippus Arideus - - - - -	7	431
Alexander Aegus - - - - -	12	443
PTOLEMY Lagus - - - - -	20	463
———— Philadelphus - - -	38	501
———— Euergetes - - - -	25	526
———— Philopater - - - -	17	543
———— Epiphanes - - - -	24	567
———— Philomater - - - -	35	602
———— Euergetes II. - - -	29	631
———— Soter - - - - - -	36	667
Dionyſius - - - - - - -	29	696
Cleopatra - - - - - - -	22	718
AUGUSTUS - - - - - - -	43	761
Tiberius - - - - - - -	22	783
Caius - - - - - - -	4	787
Claudius - - - - - - -	14	801
Nero - - - - - - -	14	815
Veſpaſian - - - - - - -	10	825

Our learned Countryman Sir John Marſham gives
this character to the Canon.—" Canon Nabonaſſaræus
ab

ab Aftronomis primùm ufurpatus, & Cœleftibus cha-
racteribus fancitus, maximam tandem auctoritatem
apud Hiftoricos non immerito obtinuit. Cujus quidem
tanta eft cum facris literis congruentia, ut fine illo vix
effet ullus ab hiftoriâ Sacrâ ad Exoticam tranfitus." p 506.
The reader is defired to take notice, 1. That this canon
is drawn up in a technical method. 2. That the Jewifh
begining of the reigns is different from that in the
canon. 3. That the angel in Daniel does not reckon
by SINGLE years, but by WEEKS of years.

[49] Sir Ifaac Newton, fpeaking of the father of
Darius the Mede mentioned Dan. ix. 1. calls him
" ACHSUERUS, ASSUERUS, OXYARES, AXERES,
prince AXERES, or CY-AXERES, the word CY figni-
fying a prince; and he adds, that the Mafforetes erro-
neoufly call him AHASUERUS. Chronol. p. 309. And
he makes ACHSCHIROSCH, ACHSURROS, or OXYARES,
the Maforetic AHASUERUS, the fame with XERXES.
p. 353. See too Jofeph Scaliger.

[50] The principle of Newton, Prideaux, &c. is
undoubtedly right when rightly applied; but in the
prefent cafe it is nothing to the purpofe. For what is
abfolutely IMPROBABLE under ONE difpenfation of
providence may be highly PROBABLE under ANOTHER.
It is therefore extremely illogical to argue from the
ORDINARY to the EXTRAORDINARY adminiftration.
And if we extend their principle to other cafes, we
fhall immediately perceive its impropriety in that before
us. Suppofe then that a queftion was put, upon the
bare narration in the book of Genefis, Whether ENOCH
WAS TRANSLATED TO HEAVEN, or DIED AN IM-

MATURE DEATH, according to the opinion of some
of the Rabbins? Here EXPERIENCE may be urged,
with much plaufibility, againft the MIRACLE; and the
confuting principle of Newton and the reft will come
in feafonably to aid and affift the objection. For
" where PROBABILITY and IMPROBABILITY appear
fo plainly upon the face of the different opinions———"
But the learned writers, as we have faid, have mifap-
plied their principle, and therefore we need not be in
any pain about the conclufion. The truth is, that the
experience of thofe who live under an ordinary providence muft be quite different from that of thofe who
live under an extraordinary one. Even the moft regu-
lar operations of Nature herfelf muft appear, miraculous fhall I fay? or improbable, to fuch as are unacquainted with them. And the good people, who always live under the influence of the warmeft fun, are
apt to fmile at the fimplicity of the northerns, when
they talk of their frozen mountains covered with ice
and fnow. Our experience is not theirs. And when
men's principles are fo very different, their conclufions
will naturally be fo too.

[51] Sir John Marfham fays, " Hæc Danielis verba,
ad ultimum Hierofolymorum excidium, a Chrifto ap-
plicantur. Matt. xxiv. 15. Ὁταν ας ιδητε το βδηλυγμα της
ερημωσιος, το ρηθεν δια Δανιηλ τε προφητε. Eft autem
παρωδια. —— Illud το ρηθεν δια τε προφητε non innuit
peculiarem a Daniele editam fuiffe prophetiam, de ca-
lamitate a Tito inferendâ; fed fignificat verba Danielis
rei, de quâ fermo eft, optimè convenire. " p. 618.
Confider the force of Chrift's words, " When ye fhall
fee THE ABOMINATION OF DESOLATION SPOKEN
OF BY DANIEL THE PROPHET, and then fay, whether

ther the deftruction of Jerufalem by Titus was foretold by Daniel, or not.

[52] " Thefe feventy weeks of Daniel are a LITTLE
PROVINCIAL KALENDAR containing the time that
the Legal worfhip and Jewifh ftate was to continue,
from the re-building of the fanctuary under Darius
Nothus until the final deftruction thereof, when the
Kalender fhould expire.——To thefe weeks therefore,
whofe computation fo efpecially concerns the Jews, is
reference made in thofe epiftles which are written to the
Chriftian churches of that nation." Mede p. 663. The
learned writer has noted feveral paffages, from which I
will felect that of St Peter, 1 ep. iv. 7. " THE END
OF ALL THINGS IS AT HAND;" furely, not the end
of the world, which has continued from Peter's time
to this. Yes, fays Baronius, for the apoftle was miftaken, as believing that the end of the world would
have happened in his own days. But —— my good
lord Cardinal ! —— give me leave to afk, If Peter
himfelf were fo very fallible, whence arifes the infal-
libility of Peter's fucceffor ?

[53] This title, we may fufpect, would offend the
Jews. Accordingly they apply to Pilate for an altera-
tion. " Write not," abfolutely, " THE KING OF
THE JEWS, but, what he himfelf faid, I AM KING
OF THE JEWS." The governor gave them a fhort
anfwer. " What I have written I have written."
" LITERA SCRIPTA MANET." And let the modern
Jews difprove the FACT, if they can.

[54] עַם נְוִיד הבא —— Few words, but full of
various fenfes. I will not trouble the reader with them,

as

as the Maforetes, Aquila, and our own tranflators have chofen that, which feems to be, beyond any reafonable doubt, the true one. Λαⲟ- ηγουμενου εϱχομενου, " the people of the prince that fhall come." Now what PRINCE can we fo reasonably fuppose to be here intended, as " PRINCE MESSIAH " fpoken of before? This fuppofition, reafonable in itfelf, is ftrengthened, if not confirmed, by the CHARACTER immediately following——" THAT SHALL COME "——one of the known characters of Meffiah. " Art thou HE THAT SHOULD COME?" was the queftion which John the Baptift put by his difciples, who doubted the Meffiah-fhip of Jefus. The character is evidently taken from Jacob's prophefy of SHILOH, and the angel's prophefy of MESSIAH. It is a very eafy thing for a critic by profeffion to embarrafs the plaineft text of fcripture. But the context will generally unravel " the fpider's web." And fo it appears to be in the prefent cafe. The prophefy fpeaks of ONE, and but ONE, eminent perfonage (THE WICKED ONE excepted) throughout. THE MOST HOLY to be ANOINTED is afterwards called MESSIAH THE PRINCE—THE MESSIAH WHO IS TO BE CUT OFF—THE COVENANTER with ALL nations—THE PRINCE THAT SHALL COME, WHOSE people fhall overthrow the city and the fanctuary, caufe the temple-fervice to ceafe, and make the land an utter defolation. And who was this, but——" JESUS OF NAZARETH THE KING OF THE JEWS?"

[55] This account of the prophecy frees it from all embarrafsment. Every thing is eafy and natural. The angel firft of all gives us the WHOLE SUM of SEVENTY WEEKS, which he afterwards divides into

THREE

THREE PARTS, SEVEN WEEKS, SIXTY-TWO WEEKS, ONE week; and then he tells us what was to be done in each period. The following feems to be the true ftate of the prophefy.

	Weeks
SEVENTY weeks are determined for thy PEOPLE and holy CITY.	70
FROM the promulgation of a commandment to rebuild Jerufalem UNTO the coming of Meffiah to deftroy it fhall be SEVEN weeks,	7
And SIXTY-TWO weeks.	62

In the SEVEN weeks, or LITTLE of thofe times, JERUSALEM SHALL BE REBUILT.

In the LATTER DAYS of the SIXTY-TWO weeks MESSIAH WILL BE CUT OFF by the Jews, and fhall caufe a NEW covenant to prevail among ALL nations, GENTILES as well as JEWS.

In HALF of ONE week HE SHALL COME in vengeance againft the Jews—by means of the ROMAN armies OVERTHROW THE CITY and THE SANCTUARY ——— thereby CAUSE THE TEMPLE-SERVICE TO CEASE for ever, and make the land defolate.

	70

[56] Some learned writers have roundly afferted, that " there is no manner of ground for underftanding an ARMY by כנף in this place. For though the Latin ALA be put for EXERCITUS, yet the Jewifh writers never ufe כנף in that fenfe." Now fuppofing, but not allowing, this to be the fact, the obfervation is nothing to the purpofe. For the paffage before us is a prediction of what was to be accomplifhed by a Roman army.

Now

Now if ALA was a term in the ROMAN tactics, then
בנף is surely the proper word to express it by in
HEBREW. And Tacitus informs us, that there were
in Titus's army, which invested Jerusalem, " octo
equitum ALÆ." Hiftor. L. v. 1.

[57] But though our Saviour forefaw, that the destruction of Jerusalem would happen in that generation,
(for it could not poffibly exceed it) yet " of that day
and hour, fays he, knoweth no one; no not the angels
of heaven," not even Gabriel, who first revealed the
great event, " neither the Son," who now again fore-
tels it, " but the Father." Mark xxxii. 32. Nor does
one text contradict the other. The time in general
might be known; the exact time, "the day and hour,"
unknown. As the Jews themfelves were to be the
inftruments in their own deftruction, it was neceffary
to fecrete the particular feafon of it. " The day and
the hour" were wifely referved in the power of God,
that it might not be in the power of man to difappoint
his purpofes.

That the latter text does, in fact, relate to the deftruction of Jerusalem, is plain from the context. " Of
THAT day and hour knoweth no one." What day
and hour? Why the day and hour included in the difciples' queftion to Jefus, " WHEN fhall thefe things
be?" his coming and the end of the age. Mat. xxiv. 3.
The Jews expected a TEMPORAL kingdom, and that
their nation, under Meffiah, would form a FIFTH
MONARCHY, and fucceed the ROMANS in the empire
of the world. They interpreted in a literal fenfe what
the prophet himfelf defigned to be underftood in a figurative one. " It fhall come to pafs IN THE LAST

DAYS,

DAYS, that the mountain of THE LORD's HOUSE shall be established in the top of the mountains, and shall be exalted above the hills, and ALL NATIONS SHALL FLOW UNTO IT." Isai. ii. 2. No sooner therefore had our Saviour mentioned the overthrow of THE TEMPLE, than they began to dream of THE KINGDOM OF ISRAEL," and that a new temple should be erected, large enough, as they foolishly conceited, for the reception of all nations. "Tell us, say they, WHEN shall these things be? and What shall be the sign of thy COMING and of the END OF THE AGE?" It is the same question, as they afterwards put to him. "Lord, wilt thou at this time grant THE KINGDOM TO ISRAEL?" And it is remarkable, that he gave them the same answer. "It is not for you to know the times or the seasons, which the Father hath put in his own power." Acts i. 6, 7.

[58] 2 Pet. i. 16—19. "We have not followed cunningly devised fables, when we made known unto you the POWER and COMING of our Lord Jesus Christ, but we have been EYE-WITNESSES of his MAJESTY, [for he received from God the Father honor and glory, when there came such a voice to him from the excellent glory, This is my beloved Son, in whom I am well pleased; and this voice which came from heaven we heared when we were with him in the holy mount] κ) ιχομεν βεβαιοτερον *, and we have a most sure word

of

* The comparative is frequently put for the superlative. So Matt. xi. 11. "He that is μικροτερω, not LESS, but LEAST in the kingdom of heaven." Ch. xviii. 1. Who is μειζων, the GREATEST in the kingdom of heaven?" 1 Cor. xiii. Μειζων, the GREATEST of these is charity." xv. 19. "If in this life only we have hope in Christ, we are of all men ελεεινοτεροι, MOST miserable." And in many other places.

of PROPHECY; whereunto ye do well that ye take heed—as unto a light that fhineth in a dark place, until the day dawn, and the day-ftar arife—in your hearts." Two things are here afferted, the POWER and the COMING of Jefus Chrift. One was paft, the other future. In proof of thefe two diftinct things he produces two diftinct teftimonies; the evidence of his own fenfes for the one, and the evidence of prophecy for the other. Here is no room for any comparifon, for what is to be compared ? The apoftle's having SEEN the MAJESTY of Jefus in the mount, was no proof that he would COME in that majefty to judge the perfecuting Jews. Nor was " the word of PROPHECY," how " fure" foever, any proof of his being at that time invefted with POWER and MAJESTY. How then can any comparifon be made between the different kinds of proof? Each was proper in its kind, and both were equally " fure." St Peter's meaning therefore is plain and obvious, and the conftruction of the paffage is this. " We have not followed a cunningly devifed fable when we made known unto you the POWER of our Lord Jefus Chrift, for we were EYE-WITNESSES of his MAJESTY. Neither have we followed a cunningly devifed fable when we made known unto you the COMING of our Lord Jefus Chrift, for we have a moft fure word of PROPHECY" relating to it. I confine this " word of prophecy" to " the feventy weeks," becaufe the apoftle is not fpeaking fimply of the coming, but of the fpeedy coming of Jefus Chrift. " THE END OF ALL THINGS IS AT HAND." 1 Pet. iv. 7. Now Daniel was the only Jewifh prophet, who had fixed the time for " THE END of the matter."

T H E   E N D.

The Reader is defired to correct the following

E R R O R S.

Page	Line	
10.	23.	*for* politically *read* fymbolically.
15.	6.	invert the commas after *of* and before *men.*
16.	13.	*for* his *read* this.
20.	28.	*read* pieces.
31.	23.	inftead of FOR *read* FOUR.
32.	4.	*read* BALYLONIANS.
63.	13.	after OBSERVATION place ''.
72.	17.	for αιωνιον read αιωνιου.
73.	18.	*for* thro' *read* through.
76.	4.	Place the [before XERXES.
—	18.	Between this line and the next *infert,* the God of Ifrael, and according to the commandment of
99.	9.	for [59] put [56]
101.	7.	for [60] put [36]
107.	21.	for Καισαρος *read* Καισαρος.
—	22.	for εγι read ηγι.
112.	4.	This line fhould be a Note at the bottom of page 113. anfwering to the reference ‡
114.	n. ‡	for ηλιον read ηλιου.
119.	15.	*for* ut *read* at.
122.	10.	for תיותא read חיותא
126.	11.	*after* himfelf *place* a comma.

www.ingramcontent.com/pod-product-compliance
Lightning Source LLC
Chambersburg PA
CBHW020010030726
47500CB00002B/525